FINAL DRAFT 1

Teacher's Manual

Series Editor: **Jeanne Lambert**
The New School

David Bohlke
Robyn Brinks Lockwood
Stanford University
Pamela Hartmann

with
Wendy Asplin, University of Washington
and
Jane Stanley McGrath

CAMBRIDGE
UNIVERSITY PRESS

CAMBRIDGE
UNIVERSITY PRESS

32 Avenue of the Americas, New York ny 10013-2473, USA

Cambridge University Press is part of the University of Cambridge.

It furthers the University's mission by disseminating knowledge in the pursuit of education, learning and research at the highest international levels of excellence.

www.cambridge.org
Information on this title: www.cambridge.org/9781107495388

First published 2016

Printed in Mexico by Editorial Impresora Apolo, S.A. de C.V.

A catalog record for this publication is available from the British Library.

ISBN 978-1-107-49535-7 Student's Book Level 1
ISBN 978-1-107-49537-1 Student's Book with Writing Skills Interactive Level 1
ISBN 978-1-107-49538-8 Teacher's Manual Level 1

Additional resources for this publication at www.cambridge.org/finaldraft

Cambridge University Press has no responsibility for the persistence or accuracy of URLs for external or third-party Internet websites referred to in this publication and does not guarantee that any content on such websites is, or will remain, accurate or appropriate. Information regarding prices, travel timetables, and other factual information given in this work is correct at the time of first printing but Cambridge University Press does not guarantee the accuracy of such information thereafter.

Art direction, book design, and photo research: emc design limited
Layout services: emc design limited

CONTENTS

INTRODUCTION

Final Draft *is a four-level academic writing series for high beginning / low intermediate- to high advanced-level students of North American English.* The series prepares students to write in a college or university setting by focusing on the topics, rhetorical modes, skills, vocabulary, and grammar necessary for students to develop their academic writing. Students are given the tools to master academic writing. First, they learn and practice foundational academic writing skills essential to writing paragraphs and essays. Then, following a process-based approach, students move through the writing process, from brainstorming with graphic organizers to organizing and developing their ideas with outlines, before completing the final draft of their unit assignment.

Final Draft *provides frequent and realistic writing models.* Each unit features writing models that reinforce the concept that writing is purposeful. The Writing in the Real World article engages students and introduces them to the topic, ideas, language, and elements of structure or rhetorical mode taught in the unit. The Student Model then demonstrates the conventions of the target structure and mode. This progression from authentic text to traditional academic writing helps students new to academic discourse first understand the purpose of communicating with a given mode before turning their attention to mastering the form.

Final Draft *focuses on key academic vocabulary.* Students need to encounter high-frequency academic vocabulary and learn how to use it naturally in preparation for college-level writing. The academic phrases and collocations in the series were selected based on the findings of research into the *Cambridge English Corpus.* Analysis of this multibillion-word collection of real-life English indicates the language that is most relevant for academic writing, with a focus here on longer lexical chunks. The academic vocabulary in the series is also corpus informed, the majority of words coming from Averil Coxhead's Academic Word List (AWL) and the remaining items taken from Michael West's General Service List (GSL). AWL words are identified as such in the index of the Student's Book.

Vocabulary items are contextualized and recycled throughout the unit. Academic collocations or academic phrases are introduced and practiced in alternating units. The writing models recycle these words and phrases in academic contexts, and in the final section of each unit students are prompted to find places where they can use these vocabulary items naturally when writing their end-of-unit assignment.

The grammar presented in **Final Draft** *is corpus informed.* Corpus research tells us the most common grammar mistakes for specific grammar points in academic writing. Students study the most common grammar mistakes drawn from the *Cambridge Learner Corpus,* a unique collection of over 50 million examples of nonnative speakers' writing. Students then work to repair them in editing activities. At the end of the unit, students are reminded to correct these mistakes as they write their assignment, which helps promote accuracy in their writing.

Final Draft *teaches students to understand and avoid plagiarism.* The series provides a robust presentation of techniques for understanding and avoiding plagiarism. Each unit includes an overview of a common plagiarism-related issue, along with a skill-building activity. This innovative approach is pedagogical, not punitive. Many ESL students struggle with a range of issues related to plagiarism. By including realistic examples and practical activities in each unit, *Final Draft* helps students avoid plagiarism and improve their academic writing.

Writing Skills Interactive *provides extra practice in key writing skills.* This online course, which can be purchased with *Final Draft,* provides graduated instruction and practice in key writing skills to help students build confidence and fluency. Each unit provides an animated presentation of the target writing skill, along with automatically graded practice activities. Each unit closes with a quiz so students can assess their progress.

Special Sections

YOUR TURN ACTIVITIES

Each unit includes a wide variety of regular writing practice activities, including Your Turn activities, which ask students to go beyond traditional practice to apply the skills, ideas, and language they have learned to their selected writing prompt. As a result, by the time they write their end-of-unit assignment, they are thoroughly prepared for the writing process because they have already practiced relevant skills and generated useful ideas and language to incorporate into their work. This makes the writing process less daunting than it would otherwise be.

Series Levels

Level	Description	CEFR Levels
Final Draft 1	Low Intermediate	A2
Final Draft 2	Intermediate	B1
Final Draft 3	High Intermediate	B2
Final Draft 4	Advanced	C1

Additional teacher resources for each level are available online at cambridge.org/finaldraft.

Final Draft 1

This book is designed for a semester-long writing course. There is enough material in the Student's Book for a course of 50 to 70 class hours. The number of class hours will vary, depending on how much of a unit is assigned outside of class and how much time a teacher decides to spend on specific elements in class. Because units are carefully designed to build toward the final writing activity, teachers are encouraged to work through each unit in chronological order. However, units can generally stand alone, so teachers can teach them in the order that best suits their needs.

Unit Overview and Teaching Suggestions

UNIT OPENER

Purpose

- To introduce the unit topic and academic discipline in an engaging way
- To elicit preliminary thinking about the unit theme and structure or rhetorical mode

Teaching Suggestion

Have students respond to the quote in writing by freewriting their ideas or by agreeing or disagreeing with the central message of the quote.

1 PREPARE YOUR IDEAS

In Section 1, students begin to explore the unit structure or rhetorical mode and choose their writing prompt for the unit.

Ⓐ Connect to Academic Writing

Purpose

- To introduce the unit structure or rhetorical mode in an accessible way
- To connect academic writing to students' lives and experience

Teaching Suggestion

To deepen the conversation, elicit additional examples from students of how the rhetorical mode connects to thinking they already do in their lives.

Ⓑ Reflect on the Topic

Purpose

- To show a writing prompt that elicits the rhetorical mode
- To introduce an appropriate graphic organizer for brainstorming and organizing ideas for the mode
- To choose a prompt for the unit writing assignment and begin generating ideas for the topic
- To engage students with the writing process early in the unit

Teaching Suggestion

Group students together who chose the same writing prompt and have them brainstorm ideas for the topic. Groups can then share their ideas with the class and receive immediate feedback.

2 EXPAND YOUR KNOWLEDGE

In Section 2, students learn academic vocabulary and read a real-world text that contains elements of the unit structure or rhetorical mode.

A Academic Vocabulary

Purpose

- To introduce high-frequency academic words from the Academic Word List and the General Service List
- To focus on the meaning of the target vocabulary within a thematic context

Teaching Suggestion

Have students choose vocabulary words from the activity that they still have trouble understanding or contextualizing and write sentences using them. They can share their sentences in groups or with the class and receive immediate feedback.

B Academic Collocations / Academic Phrases

Purpose

- To teach academic collocations and phrases that frequently occur in academic reading and writing
- To encourage the use of language chunks that will make student writing more natural and academic
- To tie academic vocabulary to the unit theme

Teaching Suggestion

Have students use the Internet to find more authentic examples of the collocations in sentences as a homework assignment. Students can then share their examples with the class or in groups.

C Writing in the Real World

Purpose

- To provide authentic content, ideas, and language in a context related to the unit theme
- To introduce elements of the unit rhetorical mode in an authentic reading
- To recycle new academic vocabulary and collocations or phrases
- To introduce features of the unit structure or mode

Teaching Suggestion

After students have read and understood the text, assign a paragraph or section to small groups, and have students work together to explain the purpose of each sentence in the section. Sample student responses: *The first sentence underlines introduces the topic, the second and third sentences give background information on the topic,* etc.

3 STUDY ACADEMIC WRITING

In Section 3, students read and analyze a student model of a traditional academic paragraph or essay. A detailed examination of elements of the unit structure or rhetorical mode follows.

Ⓐ Student Model

Purpose

- To provide an aspirational student model for the unit structure or rhetorical mode
- To deepen understanding of writing technique through real-time analysis
- To provide a context for writing skills that will be studied in Section 4
- To familiarize students with writing prompts that can be answered using the unit mode
- To recycle academic vocabulary and collocations or phrases
- To evaluate and generate more ideas on the unit theme
- To demonstrate the organization and development of ideas in traditional academic writing

Teaching Suggestion

In small groups, have students discuss their answers to the Analyze Writing Skills tasks. Then have each group present to the class on something they noticed that they found interesting or still have questions about. This offers an opportunity to deepen the discussion on writing technique.

Ⓑ Unit Structure or Rhetorical Mode

Purpose

- To deepen understanding of the unit structure or rhetorical mode
- To explain key elements of the unit structure or rhetorical mode
- To have students practice writing elements of a paragraph or essay

Teaching Suggestion

Following the activities in this section in chronological order will ensure that students have covered all the key features of the unit structure or rhetorical mode. However, if students need less work in some areas, you may want to skip those parts in class and assign the activities for homework.

In general, practice activities, including Your Turn activities, can be completed in class and immediate feedback can be given by peers or the instructor. Alternately, these sections can be assigned as homework and brought to class for review.

4 SHARPEN YOUR SKILLS

In Section 4, students review and practice key writing skills, specific applications of grammar for writing, and ways to avoid plagiarism.

Ⓐ Writing Skill

Purpose

- To provide practice with discrete writing skills that students can apply to their unit writing assignments
- To deepen knowledge of rhetorical strategies

Teaching Suggestion

Collect writing samples from one or more of the Your Turn activities in this section. Reproduce several for the class – on the board, as handouts, on a screen – to use as an editing activity.

Ⓑ Grammar for Writing

Purpose

- To present specific applications of grammar for academic writing
- To draw attention to the most common grammar mistakes made by students
- To promote grammatical accuracy in academic writing
- To improve students' editorial skills

Teaching Suggestion

After students complete the editing task at the end of the section, have students identify elements of the unit mode (e.g., language, structure) and parts of an academic paragraph (e.g., topic sentence, examples, other supporting details).

Ⓒ Avoiding Plagiarism

Purpose

- To increase awareness of the issues surrounding plagiarism
- To build skills and strategies for avoiding plagiarism
- To provide regular practice of writing skills useful for avoiding plagiarism

Teaching Suggestion

Have one student read the student question in the Q & A aloud; all other students should listen with their books closed. Elicit possible responses from the class and then compare them to the professor's answer in the book.

5 WRITE YOUR PARAGRAPH OR ESSAY

In Section 5, students go through the steps of the writing process to a final draft of their unit writing assignment.

STEP 1: BRAINSTORM

Purpose

- To brainstorm, evaluate, and organize ideas for the student paragraph or essay

Teaching Suggestion

After students brainstorm their own ideas on paper, survey the class and list the top three to five ideas for each writing prompt on the board. Then have the students explain, evaluate, and rank the ideas.

STEP 2: MAKE AN OUTLINE

Purpose

- To help students organize their paragraphs or essays before writing

Teaching Suggestion

After students complete their outlines, have them work in pairs to explain how key ideas in their outlines connect to the overall topic or thesis of their paper. This process helps confirm that their ideas are directly relevant to the topic and allows students to consider their ideas more fully.

STEP 3: WRITE YOUR FIRST DRAFT

Purpose

- To give students the opportunity to use the language, skills, and ideas from the unit to answer their writing prompt

Teaching Suggestion

After students write their first drafts, have students work in pairs to give each other feedback before turning in their writing to you. Ask partners to underline sections they think are well written and circle any words, sentences, or phrases that are unclear. Students can then revise for clarity before submitting their first drafts.

STEP 4: WRITE YOUR FINAL DRAFT

Purpose

- To evaluate and implement instructor/peer feedback
- To improve self-editing skills
- To write a final draft

Teaching Suggestion

Have students mark – highlight, underline, circle, number, etc. – sentences or parts of their writing that they revised based on peer or instructor feedback. This ensures students will incorporate some corrective feedback.

Assessment Program

The final section of the Teacher's Manual consists of an assessment program for *Final Draft*. It includes the following for each unit:

- Vocabulary quiz
- Grammar quiz
- Avoiding Plagiarism quiz
- Bank of additional writing prompts

Quizzes may be used individually or in combination with one or more of the others, depending on teacher and student needs. They are photocopiable, with downloadable versions available at cambridge.org/finaldraft. The Assessment Answer Key includes:

- General rubrics for academic writing (paragraphs / essays)
- Unit answer keys for vocabulary, grammar, and avoiding plagiarism quizzes

1 DEVELOPING IDEAS

TECHNOLOGY: COMMUNICATING IN THE MODERN WORLD

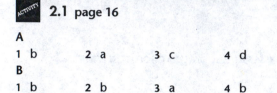

2 EXPAND YOUR KNOWLEDGE

A Academic Vocabulary page 16

 2.1 page 16

A
1 b   2 a   3 c   4 d
B
1 b   2 b   3 a   4 b

B Academic Collocations page 17

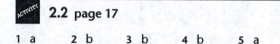 **2.2** page 17

1 a   2 b   3 b   4 b   5 a

C Writing in the Real World page 18

2.3 page 19

1 taking pictures
2 *Answers will vary. Possible answers:*
   85% of American adults own a cell phone.
   81% of women take pictures with their phones.
   80% of people text with their phones.
   13% of people over 65 access the Internet with their phones.
   70% of young adults record videos with their phones.
3 *Answers will vary. Sample answer:* "I'm a young adult, and the statistics are true for me. My friends and I text all the time, and we take lots of pictures and video with our smartphones."

 2.4 page 19

1 We use it to communicate … and to entertain.
2 For instance
3 Because

3 STUDY ACADEMIC WRITING

A Student Model page 20

1 *Answers will vary.*
2 *Answers will vary.*

Analyze Writing Skills page 20

1 <u>Nearly everyone</u> I know has a digital device such as cell phone, tablet, or laptop. OR
   <u>Using cell phones, tablets, and laptops</u> is clearly essential for socializing for my generation.
2 People like texting <u>since it's fast and easy.</u>
3 College students are also big users of social media, and this is a great way to socialize with a larger group of people.
4 For example, <u>my family lives eight hours away, so we video-chat every Saturday.</u>

 3.1 page 21

1 texting, social media, and video-chatting
2 video-chatting
3 *Answers will vary. Suggested answer:* social media.

 3.2 page 22

A Texting
   1 <u>Good for individual friends</u>
   2 <u>Fast and easy</u>
B <u>Social media</u>
   1 <u>Good for large groups of people</u>
C <u>Video-chatting</u>
   1 Good for families
   2 <u>Some families live far away</u>
   3 Writer's family lives eight hours away

B Developing Ideas page 23

 3.3 page 23

Example: A digital device such as a cell phone, tablet, or laptop is an essential tool.

Explanation: In fact, most students use some sort of digital device to get updated information on their classes from their teachers.

Reason: This saves time and allows them to share their notes with others after class.

Example: These assignments consist of online homework that teachers regularly assign.

Explanation: Some teachers only accept assignments prepared in this way, so it's very important for students to be comfortable using technology.

3.4 page 24

Answers will vary.

3.5 page 25

Answers will vary.

3.6 page 25

Answers will vary.

3.7 page 25

1 less
2 can
3 isn't

3.8 page 26

1 d   2 b   3 e   4 a   5 c

3.9 page 26

Answers will vary.

3.10 page 26

Answers will vary.

3.11 page 27

1, 4

3.12 page 28

1 no one talks to one another anymore
2 Nowadays, people accept this kind of behavior.
3 It is easy to write negative comments when we cannot see someone.
4 We often just send quick messages online.

3.13 page 29

Possible answers:
1 you don't need a building, tables, or chairs
2 it can go anywhere and sell food from there
3 they can go to a stadium, a park, or a beach

3.14 page 29

Answers will vary.

4 SHARPEN YOUR SKILLS

A Writing Skill 1: Simple and Compound Sentences page 30

4.1 page 30

A
1 I post messages on my Facebook page.
2 The food truck sells pizza and burgers.
3 Dani and Steve write a blog in the evening.
B
1 I [S] post [V] messages [O] on my Facebook page [PP].
2 The food truck [S] sells [V] pizza and burgers [CO].
3 Dani and Steve [CS] write [V] a blog [S] in the evening [PP].

4.2 page 31

1 It's easy to use Facebook, so even people uncomfortable with technology use it.
2 Jim has not joined Facebook, and his wife does not think he'll ever join.
3 You can "like" people on Facebook, or you may choose to follow people.
4 Many people still use Facebook, but some people think it will decrease in popularity.

B Writing Skill 2: Capitalization and Punctuation page 32

4.3 page 32

These days it's easy to keep in touch from the top of Mount Everest. In the past, it was hard to communicate from remote places. Edmund ¹**H**illary, the first person to reach the top of ²**E**verest, had to use heavy radio equipment to make calls. Now, both ³**C**hina and Nepal have cell-phone networks there, so people can use a cell phone. The use of GPS technology also makes things easier because climbers now know exactly where they are on the mountain. It's also easier for rescuers to find climbers who may need help. For instance, helicopters from areas ⁴**s**outh of the mountain, or from the ⁵**c**ity of ⁶**K**athmandu to the west, can quickly go in to rescue climbers during an emergency. Devices such as smartphones also help climbers get current information. It's difficult to predict the weather on Everest during the ⁷**s**ummer climbing season, but with a smartphone, climbers can get up-to-date weather forecasts. They can also send emails or post updates about their climb. The top of the world does not seem too distant these days.

4.4 page 33

1 A British climber named Daniel Hughes became famous in 2013.
2 He was the first person to use his smartphone to make a video call from Mount Everest.
3 Did he call his grandmother, his mother, or his friends?
4 He called the BBC news organization, and they interviewed him.
5 Nepal was in the news, but the government of Nepal was not happy about it.
6 Hughes did not have permission to broadcast, so the call is considered illegal.
7 The government said that Hughes would be punished for the act.
8 For example, he could face a 10-year ban from climbing Everest.

C Grammar for Writing: Simple Present page 34

 4.5 page 34

1 b, c   2 b   3 a   4 a

 4.6 page 35

1 do not trust   5 plays
2 refers   6 publish
3 lets   7 act
4 does not have   8 feel

Avoiding Common Mistakes page 36

 4.7 page 36

My uncle is a taxi driver, and he ¹**uses** technology every day in this job. He has a smartphone. The main taxi office sends him text messages that tell him where to pick up passengers. His family and friends ²**call** him regularly, too. He also has a two-way radio, but he ³**doesn't** use it very much. The main piece of technology my uncle uses is a GPS. My uncle ⁴**sometimes** does not know places in our city, so the GPS technology is very useful. The newest technology in my uncle's taxi is an information tablet for passengers. Passengers can check their route and watch the news. They can even pay for their fare using a credit card. I ⁵**think** my uncle's job has become easier with the latest technology.

D Avoiding Plagiarism page 38

 4.8 page 38

Student A
OK
Student B
Technology can change our social behavior.
In the past this was rude.
We are losing our ability to have real conversations.
Student A said where she found the information. She used her own words and did not copy exact words from the original text.

 **INTRODUCTION TO PARAGRAPHS**

PSYCHOLOGY: CHARACTERISTICS OF SUCCESS

2 EXPAND YOUR KNOWLEDGE

A Academic Vocabulary page 46

 2.1 page 46

A
1 a   2 d   3 b   4 c
B
1 d   2 a   3 b   4 c

B Academic Phrases page 47

 2.2 page 47

1 One of the most important
2 Part of the problem
3 It is important

C Writing in the Real World page 48

 2.3 page 49

1 *Answers will vary.*
2 b, c, e, f
3 *Answers will vary.*

2.4 page 49

1 Felix could not have done his successful space jump on his own.
2 3
3 Success requires the help and support of other people.

3 STUDY ACADEMIC WRITING

Ⓐ Student Model page 50

Analyze Writing Skills page 50

1 <u>There are three parts of my life I want to be successful at.</u>
2 First
3 <u>Second, I want to be really good at playing the guitar. I do not want to be in a band or to play professionally, but I would like to play for fun.</u> For example, I would like to play guitar for my family and friends when we are all together.
4 Third
5 In conclusion

3.1 page 51

1 successful at career, playing the guitar, successful with money and have no debt
2 *Answers will vary.*
3 *Answers will vary.*

3.2 page 52

A Career
  1 Be a doctor who really helps people
  2 <u>Spend time with patients</u>
B Playing guitar
  1 <u>Not in band, play for fun</u>
  2 <u>Play for friends and family</u>
C <u>Finances</u>
  1 Grew up poor
  2 <u>Never had new clothes, had to borrow money</u>

Ⓑ The Paragraph page 52

3.3 page 52

1 are related
2 always
3 similar

3.4 page 53

1 SS   2 CS   3 TS   4 SS   5 SS
Successful students share three characteristics. First, successful students get good grades. They study hard and earn high marks in their classes. They usually win awards. Also, successful students do extracurricular activities. For example, they play on one of the school's sports teams, are a member of a club, or play an instrument in the school band. Finally, successful students have excellent attendance. They rarely miss classes, even when they feel tired. In conclusion, there are several characteristics that successful students share.

3.5 page 53

1 My greatest personal success was <u>teaching my brother how to ride a bike.</u>
2 There are <u>benefits</u> to failing before you succeed.
3 One of the most successful people I know is my father.
4 <u>Bill Gates</u> is one of the most successful businessmen in history.
5 There are <u>three strategies</u> to successfully learn a second language.
6 Being successful requires a <u>team of people.</u>
7 I believe you can learn <u>three lessons</u> from failing before you succeed.
8 The most popular videos on YouTube share <u>several characteristics.</u>

3.6 page 54

Possible answers:
1 Successful parents share several characteristics.
2 Success changes people by making them stronger.
3 Achieving your goals requires hard work and intelligence.
4 Failure can be a good thing because it can make people stronger.
5 Many people think that success does not come naturally; I think it takes a good education, family support, and a desire to do well.

3.7 page 55

Answers will vary.

3.8 page 57

1, 2, 3, 4, 5

3.9 page 57

First, to be successful you need a clear goal.
Second, being successful requires focus.
Third, being successful requires confidence.

 3.10 page 57

Possible answers:

1 A movie should have lots of action.
2 A movie needs to have an interesting plot.
3 A good movie must have popular actors that people want to go see.

 3.11 page 58

1 b   2 c   3 a

 3.12 page 58

Answers will vary.

 3.13 page 58

Answers will vary.

 3.14 page 59

1 c   2 c   3 b

 3.15 page 60

Answers will vary. Possible answer: In conclusion, planning in advance can help you have a great vacation.

 3.16 page 60

Answers will vary.

4 SHARPEN YOUR SKILLS

Ⓐ Writing Skill 1: Writing Good Topic Sentences page 61

 4.1 pages 61–62

1 S, B, G   4 G, B, S
2 G, S, B   5 S, B, G
3 B, S, G

 4.2 page 62

Answers will vary.

 4.3 page 63

Answers will vary. Possible answer: Failure often comes before success, and several famous people illustrate this.

Ⓑ Writing Skill 2: Titles page 64

 4.4 page 64

1 U   3 A   5 U
2 U   4 U   6 A

 4.5 page 65

Answers will vary. Possible answers:
1 Benefits of Working Part-Time
2 Careful Planning Leads to Success
3 A Child's Greatest Influence

Ⓒ Grammar for Writing: Common Verb + Preposition Combinations page 66

 4.6 page 66

A
1 work for
2 look for
3 commit to
4 focuses on
B
1 takes care of
2 learn from
3 get ahead of
4 cares about

Avoiding Common Mistakes page 67

 4.7 page 67

Success does not mean winning all the time. There are some very successful people who failed before becoming famous and successful. They stayed committed ¹**to** their goals and kept trying. The first example is Steve Jobs. When Jobs was younger, he was fired from Apple, the company he started. However, he stayed focused ²**on** business. He started another company, bought a movie company, and invented some of the electronics millions of people use today. The second example is Walt Disney. Walt Disney worked ³**for** a newspaper. He was fired because the manager did not think he had enough imagination or original ideas. Despite this failure, Walt Disney focused ⁴**on** his goal and proved that he had a lot of imagination by starting Disneyland, Disney World, and EPCOT. People think he was one of the most creative people who ever lived. The third example is Oprah Winfrey. She was a news anchor for a television station. The managers did not like her work. They said she cried too much and did not look good on television. She did not let the failure stop her ⁵**from** achieving success. Later, her talk show was one of the most-watched shows on television. In conclusion, even some of the most successful people have failed on their road to success.

ⓓ Avoiding Plagiarism page 68

 4.8 page 68

Answers will vary.

 NARRATIVE PARAGRAPHS

HEALTH: HEALTH BEHAVIORS

2 EXPAND YOUR KNOWLEDGE

ⓐ Academic Vocabulary page 76

 2.1 page 76

1 b	3 b	5 b	7 a
2 a	4 a	6 b	8 a

ⓑ Academic Collocations page 77

 2.2 page 77

1 d   2 c   3 a   4 e   5 b

ⓒ Writing in the Real World page 78

 2.3 page 79

1 getting enough sleep
2 good physical health; clear thinking; prevent emotional problems
3 four

 2.4 page 79

1 importance of sleep
2 b; "as a child"
3 sleep

3 STUDY ACADEMIC WRITING

ⓐ Student Model page 80

Analyze Writing Skills page 80

1 a heart attack
2 I was overweight when I was growing up, and my quality of life was terrible. All I did was relax at home, eat, and play video games. I was very unhealthy. My father was unhealthy, too. Like me, he was overweight and did not exercise.
3 After he came home from the hospital, we decided to make significant improvements to our quality of life.
4 my dad saved my life

 3.1 page 81

1 They were both unfit and overweight.
2 His dad had a heart attack. They started eating better and exercising. They both lost weight.
3 *Answers will vary.*

3.2 pages 81–82

A Overweight and did not exercise
  1 Just relaxed, ate, and played video games
  2 Father was unhealthy too
  3 Quality of life terrible
B Father's heart attack
  1 Big shock
  2 Got healthy together
C Got healthy again
  1 Started eating well
  2 Started walking, then running
  3 Vegetables, chicken, and fish
  4 Lost over 250 pounds

B **Narrative Paragraphs** page 82

 3.3 page 82

5, 3, 4, 6, 8, 1, 7, 2

 3.4 page 83

1 at the beginning
2 second
3 fifth

 3.5 page 84

1 b, a   2 a, b   3 a, b

 3.6 page 84

Answers will vary.

 3.7 page 85

One day; At that time; First; After a while; Then;
Later; Finally; The next day

 3.8 page 86

Answers will vary.

 3.9 page 87

Answers will vary. Possible answers: The hike was
only two miles; We walked for an hour; All our
muscles hurt.

 3.10 page 87

Answers will vary.

 3.11 page 88

1 She knew she could dance again.
2 … was change our attitude.
3 … the importance of following directions.

 3.12 page 88

Answers will vary.

 3.13 page 88

Answers will vary.

4 SHARPEN YOUR SKILLS

A **Writing Skill 1: Complex Sentences**
  page 89

 4.1 pages 89–90

1 a; Because Lili never had much time in the
  morning, she just had coffee for breakfast. OR
  Lili just had coffee for breakfast because she
  never had much time in the morning.
2 b; Lili soon felt hungry and had no energy
  because she did not have a nutritious breakfast.
  OR Because Lili did not have a nutritious
  breakfast, she soon felt hungry and had no
  energy.
3 b; Lili decided to have a complete breakfast
  every morning because her work was suffering.
  OR Because Lili's work was suffering, she
  decided to have a complete breakfast every
  morning.
4 b; There was a significant improvement in her
  energy each day because she began the day with
  a good breakfast. OR Because Lili began the day
  with a good breakfast, there was a significant
  improvement in her energy each day.

 4.2 page 91

1 When a new diet trend appears, people get
  very excited. OR People get very excited when
  a new diet trend appears.
2 There were the "low-fat diets" of the 1980s
  before the "low-sugar diets" of today appeared.
  OR Before the "low-sugar diets" of today
  appeared, there were the "low-fat diets" of
  the 1980s.
3 After a movie star recommends a diet trend,
  many people change what they eat. OR Many
  people change what they eat after a movie star
  recommends a diet trend.

B Writing Skill 2: Avoiding Sentence Fragments page 91

 4.3 page 92

Ordered fish, vegetables, and a glass of wine.;
The man Jack LaLanne!; When I was young.;
He 92 years old.; If you want to stay healthy always.;
It a good, long life.

C Grammar for Writing: Pronouns page 93

 4.4 page 94

1 Some of my classmates do not worry about <u>their</u> health. Right now, <u>they</u> just want to have a good time and enjoy <u>themselves</u>.
2 We are a team of athletes. <u>We</u> commit <u>ourselves</u> to daily exercise, but <u>we</u> also believe that nutrition and sleep are important to <u>our</u> health. We rely on <u>each other / one another</u> during a race, so being fit is important.
3 Maria walks three miles a day and works in <u>her</u> garden on weekends. <u>She</u> grows <u>her</u> own tomatoes, carrots, broccoli, and strawberries.
4 John tries to eat well, but sometimes <u>he</u> eats junk food because <u>it</u> is fast and easy. <u>He</u> takes multi-vitamin pills every day. <u>They</u> give him the vitamins that are not in <u>his</u> diet.

Avoiding Common Mistakes page 94

 4.5 page 95

Recently, my grandmother ¹**she** decided not to pay attention to medical science. When she was young, she read all the new health studies. At that time, she learned that fat was bad for us. That's why she started to buy only nonfat milk and low-fat cheese. However, a few months ago, she read about a new study. This study ²**it** said that fat is *not* a problem. Instead, *sugar* is the big problem. When she was young, coffee and chocolate were "bad." Now both are good. Then there was research about calcium. For many years, my grandmother took a calcium pill every day for ³**her** bones because doctors ⁴**they** said it was important. Now they say to get calcium from food only – not a pill. Thirty years ago, her husband hurt ⁵**his** back. Doctors told him to stay in bed and rest. Later, doctors told him the same thing after ⁶**he** had a heart attack. These days, doctors say to get up and move. My grandmother is furious.

Last week, she went to see her doctor. In a shopping bag, she had many magazines with articles about health. Now my grandmother does not pay attention to medical news because ⁷**it** changes all the time. These days, she eats anything she wants and waits for medical science to change its mind.

D Avoiding Plagiarism page 96

 4.6 page 97

✓ 1 The U.S. Civil War was a fight between the North and the South.
✓ 2 The largest mammal in the world is the blue whale.
☐ 3 Memorizing words is not a good way to learn English.
☐ 4 Harvard has almost 52,000 alumni in over 200 countries.
✓ 5 Muhammad Ali was one of the world's great heavyweight boxing champions.

④ PROCESS PARAGRAPHS

BUSINESS: GETTING AHEAD

2 EXPAND YOUR KNOWLEDGE

A Academic Vocabulary page 104

 2.1 page 104

A
1 d   2 b   3 a   4 c
B
1 b   2 a   3 b   4 b

B Academic Phrases page 105

 2.2 page 105

1 b   2 b   3 c

C Writing in the Real World page 106

 2.3 page 107

1 answered the phone
2 b, e
3 *Answers will vary.*

2.4 page 107

1 6 a, 3 b, 5 c, 2 d, 1 e, 4 f
2 *Answers will vary.*

3 STUDY ACADEMIC WRITING

A Student Model page 108

Analyze Writing Skills page 108

1 [1] The first step is to approach the customer and let them know your role.
2 c
3 [2] Second, find out; [3] Next, explain; [4] After that, be; [5] Finally, bring

 3.1 page 109

1 1. Approach the customer and let them know your role, 2. Find out about the customer's needs, 3. Explain the key features of the product, 4. Be available for questions, 5. Bring the customer to the check-out counter.
2 *Answers will vary.*
3 *Answers will vary.*

 3.2 page 110

A 1 Remember to smile
B Find out about needs by asking questions
B 2 Stay nearby customers who are "just looking"
C Explain product's key features
D Be available for questions
E 1 An opportunity to sell more

B Process Paragraphs page 111

 3.3 page 112

If you follow these five simple steps.

 3.4 page 112

1 b   2 b   3 a

 3.5 page 113

Answers will vary.

 3.6 page 113

Answers will vary.

 3.7 page 114

Step 1: First, get a part-time job in the field.
Step 2: After that, learn all you can while trying to get noticed by people in the field.
Step 3: Next, apply to a culinary arts school.
Step 4: Finally, think about exactly what you want to do in the field of culinary arts.

 3.8 page 115

1 c   2 d   3 b   4 e   5 a

 3.9 page 115

3 c   5 d   2 e   4 a   1 b

 3.10 page 116

Answers will vary.

 3.11 page 117

Answers will vary.

 3.12 page 117

These steps are not difficult and, in time, they will help you get that job interview.

 3.13 page 117

Answers will vary.

 3.14 pages 117–118

Answers will vary.

4 SHARPEN YOUR SKILLS

A Writing Skill 1: Transitions of Sequential Order page 119

4.1 page 119

1 First of all,
2 Next/Then/After that,
3 Next/Then/After that,
4 Next/Then/After that,
5 Lastly

B Writing Skill 2: Adding Details

page 120

 4.2 page 120

Answers will vary.

C Grammar for Writing: Imperatives

page 121

 4.3 page 121

1 get
2 brainstorm
3 Remember / Don't forget
4 remove
5 look at
6 test
7 choose
8 Don't forget / Remember

Avoiding Common Mistakes page 122

 4.4 page 122

How to Make Coffee at Work
Anyone can make coffee in just five steps in our office pantry. First, fill the pot with water. ¹**Do not** fill it with hot water – always use cold water. Then take a coffee filter, ²~~you~~ fill it with some coffee, and place the filter and coffee into the coffee maker. Next, pour the water carefully into the coffee maker. ³**Do not** spill it! After that place the empty pot on the burner under the filter and turn it on. Leave the coffee there until it is done. Finally, ⁴~~you~~ enjoy your coffee. When the coffee pot is empty, ⁵**do not** forget to empty the filter and wash the pot for the next person. See what an easy process coffee making can be!

D Avoiding Plagiarism page 123

4.5 page 124

A
1 b, d
2 a, g
3 h, f
4 e, c
B
businesses and working mothers

 ⑤ DEFINITION PARAGRAPHS

EDUCATION: THE VALUE OF EDUCATION

2 EXPAND YOUR KNOWLEDGE

A Academic Vocabulary page 132

 2.1 pages 132–133

A
1 a   2 b   3 a   4 b
B
1 c   2 d   3 b   4 a

B Academic Collocations

 2.2 page 133

1 b   2 a   3 b   4 a   5 b

C Writing in the Real World page 134

 2.3 page 135

1 increased salary; *answers will vary*
2 *Answers will vary.*
3 *Answers will vary.*

2.4 page 135

1 job satisfaction, is defined as
2 job stability, means
3 *Answers will vary.*

3 STUDY ACADEMIC WRITING

A Student Model page 136

Analyze Writing Skills page 136
1 Vocational schools are <u>a type of school which provide career training.</u>
2 <u>Vocational schools are not universities.</u>
3 At a vocational school, students study two years or less, and they focus on a single field, such as health services, flower design, or car repair. The businesses spend time and money training students, so graduates can expect to get a good job there.
4 This is extremely beneficial for people who <u>want to get a job after they graduate.</u>

3.1 page 137

1 *Answers will vary.*
2 short course of study, focus on a single field, get work experience from local businesses, local businesses hire graduates
3 *Answers will vary.*

 3.2 page 138

Definition: <u>A type of school that provides career training</u>

A <u>Similar to community colleges</u>
   1 Because they offer short programs
   2 Not universities
B <u>Focus on a single field</u>
   1 <u>Health services, flower design, or car repair</u>
   2 Advantage for students who know what they want to do
C Good for people interested in changing or finding new careers
   1 <u>Someone who is unhappy in his job</u>
   2 Someone who raised kids
D <u>Have close connections with businesses</u>
   1 Can get work experience
   2 Can get job right away

ⓑ Definition in Academic Writing
  page 139

 3.3 page 140

Paragraph 1; that

 3.4 page 141

1 Tutors are <u>private teachers</u> <u>who often teach students one on one.</u>
2 A transcript is <u>an official document</u> <u>that lists all your classes and grades.</u>
3 A thesaurus is <u>a reference book</u> <u>that has words with the same meaning grouped together.</u>
4 The dictionary defines a teaching assistant as <u>a person</u> <u>who assists a professor with his or her class.</u>

 3.5 page 141

Answers will vary.

 3.6 page 141

Answers will vary.

 3.7 page 142

Answers will vary.

 3.8 page 143

1 b   2 a   3 b   4 a

 3.9 page 143

1 b   2 d   3 a   4 e   5 c

 3.10 page 144

Suggested answers:
1 A group project teaches the importance of collaborations.
2 I was part of a group project in high school. We planned the senior dance.
3 A group project is similar to pair work.
4 A group project is not a project you do by yourself.

 3.11 page 144

Answers will vary.

 3.12 page 145

Answers will vary.

4 SHARPEN YOUR SKILLS

ⓐ Writing Skill: Paragraph Unity
  page 146

 4.1 page 146

The irrelevant sentence is: Some teachers say they don't like to correct homework.

ⓑ Grammar for Writing: Subject Relative Clauses page 147

 4.2 page 147

1 which   3 which   5 who
2 who   4 who   6 which

4.3 page 148

1 Home schooling is a type of education that takes place at home rather than in a school.
2 Home schooling is an option which/that is becoming more and more popular.
3 A home-schooling parent is a teacher who is also a principal, a coach, a cook, and an administrator.
4 A home-schooler is a type of student who studies at home instead of at school.
5 State schools are places of learning which/that sometimes have a poor learning environment.

Avoiding Common Mistakes page 149

 4.4 page 149

In North America, a major is a specific subject ¹**which** a student studies while working toward a college degree. Typically between a third and half of a student's courses are part of his or her major. The other courses are known as core courses. These consist of classes that all students ²**they** have to take. Students usually need to choose a major by the end of their second year of study. Students who ³**want** to can also choose two majors. This is called a double major. This is an advantage for students ⁴**who** can't decide between two majors. Another option is choosing a major and a minor. A minor is similar to a major. It's also a specific subject area ⁵**which/that** a student studies, but students need to take fewer classes to achieve a minor. Choosing a major is clearly an important part of the college experience.

D Avoiding Plagiarism page 150

 4.5 page 150

College education has many advantages. According to Lizzie Wann, Content Director for Bridgeport Education, one of the most important advantages is passing on the legacy. She says that if a person graduates from college, that person's children will probably enjoy a better quality of life and pursue extended education themselves. Also, it will be easier for them to get into better schools if their mother or father has made it clear how important it is to get an education.

6 DESCRIPTIVE PARAGRAPHS

CULTURAL STUDIES: CULTURAL LANDMARKS

2 EXPAND YOUR KNOWLEDGE

A Academic Vocabulary page 158

 2.1 page 158

1 a	3 b	5 b	7 b
2 b	4 b	6 b	8 a

B Academic Phrases page 159

 2.2 page 159

1 c   2 a   3 b

C Writing in the Real World page 160

 2.3 page 161

1 They are similar in that they are both tombs.
2 We know builders designed it to allow people to study the sky. We believe Stonehenge was a place for religious ceremonies. These ceremonies let people remember their ancestors.
3 *Answers will vary.*

2.4 page 161

1 Today, the Taj Mahal is a symbol of India, but it also symbolizes love. In the seventeenth century, Shah Jahan built the beautiful buildings and gardens, at great cost, as a tomb for his deceased wife. At the center is the brilliant white dome, which rises high above the area. At the top of this dome is a lotus flower, another symbol of India, and around this large dome are four smaller ones. Exquisite decoration and Islamic writing cover the buildings.
The most important part is probably the "beautiful white dome" because it is "at the center" and "rises high above the area." However, some students might say the lotus flower is most important because it is at the top of the dome and is a symbol of India.
2 at the center, above the area, at the top of this dome, around this large dome

3 STUDY ACADEMIC WRITING

Ⓐ Student Model page 162

Analyze Writing Skills page 162

1 The flag of Malaysia is a famous symbol of my country. It is beautiful and colorful.
2 at the top; on the left
3 In the middle of the blue area is a big yellow star and a crescent moon.
4 big yellow

 3.1 page 163

1 14 / They represent the states and the government.
2 People of Malaysia are from different cultures, and they have different religions. However, they try to work together. / He feels proud.
3 A big yellow star and a crescent moon. Yellow is the color of the king and queen. The moon is a religious symbol. It symbolizes Islam, which is the religion of Malaysia.

 3.2 page 163

A Beautiful and colorful
  1 Red, white, blue, and yellow
B Fourteen red and white stripes
  1 Represent the states and the government
C Blue rectangle
  1 Color symbolizes unity
  2 Different people try to work together
D Yellow star and crescent moon
  1 Yellow = color of the king and queen
  2 Moon = religious symbol (= Islam)

Ⓑ Descriptive Paragraphs page 164

 3.3 pages 164–165

1 visitors, religious landmark
2 tourist, spend the day
3 famous, not like
4 people, cultural landmark, think of/about

 3.4 page 165

1 c
2 b

 3.5 page 166

Answers will vary.

 3.6 page 167

1 In the middle   4 in front of
2 On the left   5 At the bottom
3 next to   6 Behind

 3.7 page 168

Answers will vary.

 3.8 page 169

biggest to smallest

 3.9 page 169

Answers will vary.

 3.10 page 169

Answers will vary.

 3.11 page 170

1 c, d   3 f   5 b
2 a   4 e

 3.12 page 171

Answers will vary.

 3.13 page 171

Answers will vary.

 3.14 page 171

c

3.15 page 171

Answers will vary.

4 SHARPEN YOUR SKILLS

Ⓐ Writing Skill: Adding Details with Adjectives and Adverbs page 172

 4.1 page 172

1 famous <u>symbol</u>; <u>is</u>; beautiful <u>statue</u>; <u>is</u>; huge (<u>statue</u>); relaxed <u>hands</u>; <u>are</u>; <u>is</u>; tight <u>curls</u>; <u>looks</u>; peaceful (<u>face</u>); religious <u>importance</u>
2 incredible <u>landmark</u>; <u>is</u>; 16th century; <u>is</u>; colorful <u>collection</u>; bright red, green, blue, yellow, gold <u>colors</u>; interesting <u>characteristic</u>; beautiful <u>domes</u>; <u>look</u>

 4.2 page 173

<u>relax</u> lazily; <u>sit</u> sleepily; <u>talk</u> quietly; <u>sits</u> happily; comfortably … <u>lived</u>

 4.3 page 173

1 small
2 strong-looking
3 long
4 ancient
5 beautifully; completely

 4.4 page 173

Answers will vary.

Ⓑ Grammar for Writing: *There is* and *There are* page 174

 4.5 page 174

A
1 there are
2 There are
3 there is
4 There are
5 there is
6 There is
B
On the left; in front of; At the top; on the right; in the background

Avoiding Common Mistakes page 175

 4.6 page 175

In the state of South Dakota, [1]**there** is a huge stone monument. It is at the top of a mountain in the beautiful Black Hills. On this mountain, [2]**there** are the massive heads of U.S. presidents. [3]**There** are four of them: George Washington, Thomas Jefferson, Theodore Roosevelt, and Abraham Lincoln. This monument is a popular place for people on vacation. [4]**There are** almost three million people who visit the area each year. However, not everyone enjoys this monument. [5]**There are** many Native Americans who are unhappy about it. For them, this land has cultural and religious importance.

Ⓒ Avoiding Plagiarism page 176

 4.7 page 177

1 This is an example of plagiarism. Roberto did not use his own ideas.
2 This is an example of plagiarism. Susie reused a writing assignment for another class.
3 This is an example of plagiarism. Carol is using a paragraph that she did not write.
4 This is not an example of plagiarism. Mei moved beyond the group discussion to come up with and write her own ideas.

⑦ OPINION PARAGRAPHS

GENERAL STUDIES: POPULAR CULTURE

2 EXPAND YOUR KNOWLEDGE

Ⓐ Academic Vocabulary page 184

2.1 page 184

A
1 b   2 a   3 d   4 c
B
1 a   2 c   3 d   4 b

B Academic Collocations page 185

 2.2 page 185

1 a   2 c   3 b   4 e   5 d

C Writing in the Real World page 186

 2.3 page 187

1 for children to not look after their elderly parents
2 the population of elderly is growing and not as many elderly people live with their children anymore
3 *Answers will vary.*

 2.4 page 187

1 Some people believe … ,
2 five
3 *Answers will vary.*

3 STUDY ACADEMIC WRITING

A Student Model page 188

Analyze Writing Skills page 188

1 in my opinion, childhood is the best
2 First
3 Another reason
4 Finally, the most important reason
5 For these reasons

 3.1 page 189

1 children have more free time than adults; children have stronger friendships; children have loving family members who want to take care of them; children do not have to go to work
2 *Answers will vary.*

 3.2 page 190

A More free time
  1 lots of time for fun
  2 students spend 180 days in school
B Stronger friendships
  1 spend more time with friends than adults
  2 psychologists: children's friendships are better

C children are taken care of
  1 Happy birthday parties
D children do not work
  1 15% of American adults hate their jobs
  2 School better than working all day

B Opinion Writing page 191

 3.3 page 192

1 O   3 F   5 O   7 O
2 F   4 F   6 F

 3.4 page 192

Answers will vary.

 3.5 page 193

I think that; In my opinion

 3.6 page 193

Suggested words to underline:
1 parents, teachers
2 media, attention, celebrities / public figures

 3.7 page 193

Answers will vary.

 3.8 page 194

1 First
2 Another reason is
3 The most important reason is

 3.9 page 195

Answers will vary.

 3.10 page 196

Answers will vary.

 3.11 page 196

Answers will vary.

 3.12 page 196

Answers will vary.

3.13 page 197

money, athletes, justified

 3.14 page 197

1 SS   2 SS   3 SS   4 CS   5 TS

 3.15 page 197

5, 3, 1, 2, 4

4 SHARPEN YOUR SKILLS

Ⓐ Writing Skill 1: Formal vs. Informal Language page 198

 4.1 page 198

IMO – In my opinion
b/c – because
wanna – want to
don't – do not
hafta – have to

 4.2 page 199

Answers will vary.

Ⓑ Writing Skill 2: Word Forms page 199

 4.3 page 200

Noun	Adjective	Verb	Adverb
suggestion	*suggestive*	*suggest*	*suggestively*
illegality	*Illegal*	*–*	*illegally*
information	*informative*	*inform*	*informatively*
greatness	*great*	*–*	*greatly*
entertainment	*entertaining*	*entertain*	*entertainingly*
relation	*related*	*relate*	*relatedly*
personality	*personal*	*personalize*	*personally*

 4.4 page 200

1 believe (v)
2 influential (adj)
3 personal (adj)
4 information (n)
5 quickly (adv)
6 recently (adv)
7 strongly (adv)

Ⓒ Grammar for Writing: Superlatives
page 201

 4.5 page 201

1 the most successful
2 the worst
3 the most interesting
4 the cheapest
5 the most violent
6 the healthiest

Avoiding Common Mistakes page 202

4.6 page 202

In my opinion, college should be free for all students. First, free education is the [1]**best** way to help the economy in the future. Having the [2]**most** smartest people will make our country the most [3]**competitive** in the world. We would have the [4]**best** doctors, engineers, or teachers. Another reason is because it makes society more equal. Some really talented people, like my friend Asher, cannot go to college because they do not have enough money. Free college means everyone who is accepted can go, no matter how much money they have. This is true in Denmark, which is one of the [5]**happiest** places to live. Finally, it is wrong to burden people with huge debt at such a young age. According to research, graduates in the U.S.A. have almost $30,000 in loan debt. For some people, it is the [6]**most expensive** mistake they make. For these reasons, I believe a college education should be free.

Ⓓ Avoiding Plagiarism page 203

4.7 page 204

1 According to Carolyn Foote, all of us "set examples for our children every day."
2 Carolyn Foote says, "We want every child to succeed."
3 Foote asks, "But do we want to show our students that success at any cost is the goal?"

INTRODUCTION TO ESSAYS

HUMAN RESOURCES: CAREER PATHS

2 EXPAND YOUR KNOWLEDGE

A Academic Vocabulary page 212

 2.1 page 212

1 a	3 a	5 b	7 a
2 b	4 b	6 a	8 a

B Academic Phrases page 213

2.2 page 213

1 c   2 a   3 b

C Writing in the Real World page 214

2.3 page 215

1 Picasso painted until the day he died; To show how passionate he was about his job
2 extrinsic, lifestyle, intrinsic; to discover their values.

2.4 page 215

job, career, choose

3 STUDY ACADEMIC WRITING

A Student Model page 216

Analyze Writing Skills pages 216–217
1 My objective is to become a photojournalist because it is important for me to be creative, have exciting experiences, and learn new things.
2 In addition, the job has excitement and adventure.
3 In conclusion,
4 same

3.1 page 217

1 Most of the adults were not happy in their work.
2 The writer wants his career to make him happy.
3 to be creative, have exciting experiences, and learn new things

 3.2 page 218

I Introductory paragraph
  A Why do some people spend their adult life doing a job they hate?
  B Adults in my life not happy in their work
  C My objective is to become a photojournalist because it is important for me to be creative.
II A creative job
  A Works with a photojournalist to tell a story
    1 Reporter uses words, photojournalist uses photos
    2 Photo essays
III Excitement/adventure
  A No need to sit at a desk
  B Do job in many different places
    1 Famous person, nature photos
IV Opportunity to learn new things
  A Subjects
    1 Music, science, politics
V Concluding paragraph
  A Follow these values, not spend my life complaining about my work

B From Paragraphs to Essays page 219

3.3 page 220

1 Why do some people spend their adult life doing a job they hate?
2 question
3 When I was growing up, most of the adults in my life were not happy in their work. In general, they worked only because they needed the salary and health benefits. They wanted job security, but they worked all day and were bored. To be honest, I never understood this about adults. I decided to find a career to make me happy.
4 personal story
5 My objective is to become a photojournalist because it is important for me to be creative, have exciting experiences, and learn new things.

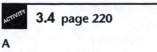

3.4 page 220

A

a	5	c	2	e	6
b	3	d	1	f	4

B

Most people spend 60% of their life working. Sixty percent means that these people spend more time at work than with friends or family. Because we spend so much time with them, people in the workplace are very important in our lives. Poor relationships at work can cause stress and unhappiness in life in general. However, good workplace relationships can make us much happier. For a happier life, it is important to encourage good relationships with supervisors, co-workers, and employees.

3.5 page 221

Suggested answers:

1 Not good; It does not answer the prompt.
2 Good
3 Not good; It does not have three aspects in the point of view.

3.6 page 222

Suggested answers:

1 I will know that I am a success when I have control over my own schedule, own my own business, and have a sense of achievement.
2 In my opinion, money is important because it provides us with basic needs, allows us to support our family members, and lets us help other people in society.
3 I think it is important to spend time outside work on physical exercise, spiritual growth, and relationships with friends and family.

3.7 page 222

Answers will vary.

3.8 page 223

1 <u>In addition</u>, the job has excitement and adventure.
2 I will not have to sit at a desk and do the same job eight hours every day. Instead, each day will be different and exciting.

3 This is because I can perform my job in all sorts of places.
4 I will take photos of famous people who are filming a movie; I will take nature photos of oceans and the animals in them; I hope to travel around the world and see other cultures.

3.9 page 224

A

A	3	B	1	C	2

B

Answers will vary.

3.10 page 224

Answers will vary.

3.11 page 226

Answers will vary.

3.12 page 226

b

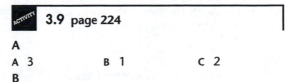

4 SHARPEN YOUR SKILLS

Ⓐ Writing Skill: Avoiding Run-on Sentences and Comma Splices
page 227

4.1 pages 227–228

A

A good nanny must be very **patient children** do things that can drive adults crazy. Some babies cry for hours. At the age of two, a child's favorite word is "No." Children can also get very **angry they** throw themselves on the floor and cry. Some children ask a lot of questions. Some children want the nanny to read the same story to them over and over. Many adults do not have the patience for **this, a** good nanny has a lot of patience.

A good nanny must also be a creative thinker. A nanny needs to create activities that children like. Children enjoy **surprises, they** like to discover things. Also, it is essential for a nanny to think of ways to solve **problems, the** nanny is often alone all day with the children. The parents are not there to give **directions the** nanny must take responsibility for things that go wrong.

The third characteristic of a good nanny is the ability to multitask. In a home with several children, many things happen at the same time. The nanny must be able to cook dinner for older children with one **hand with** another hand she feeds the baby. With her third hand, she helps a child with **homework, with** her fourth hand, she plays a game with another child. As you see, it is necessary for a nanny to have many hands.

B

Possible answer:

A good nanny must be very **patient because children** do things that can drive adults crazy. Some babies cry for hours. At the age of two, a child's favorite word is "No." Children can also get very **angry. They** throw themselves on the floor and cry. Some children ask a lot of questions. Some children want the nanny to read the same story to them over and over. Many adults do not have the patience for **this, but a** good nanny has a lot of patience.

A good nanny must also be a creative thinker. A nanny needs to create activities that children like. Children enjoy **surprises, and they** like to discover things. Also, it is essential for a nanny to think of ways to solve **problems because the** nanny is often alone all day with the children. The parents are not there to give **directions, so the** nanny must take responsibility for things that go wrong.

The third characteristic of a good nanny is the ability to multitask. In a home with several children, many things happen at the same time. The nanny must be able to cook dinner for older children with one **hand, and with** another hand she feeds the baby. With her third hand, she helps a child with **homework. With** her fourth hand, she plays a game with another child. As you see, it is necessary for a nanny to have many hands.

B Grammar for Writing: Parallel Structure page 228

 4.2 page 228

Possible answers:

1 A nanny cooks dinner, feeds the baby, **helps with homework**, and plays games.
2 The world is very different from 100 years ago because of advances in technology, education, and **healthcare**.
3 It is a chance to learn about subjects such as music, science, politics, and **religion**.

4 Happiness comes from achievement and **creativity**.
5 My work environment is enjoyable, fun, and **friendly**.

Avoiding Common Mistakes page 229

 4.3 page 229

In the past, most people had no opportunity to choose their own career. They did the same work as their parents, were hired as apprentices, or [1]**were given work by the landowner**. If a father was a farmer, the son had to stay and farm, too. If the king picked someone for his army, the person became a soldier. Most women had to stay home. They had to cook meals, clean clothes [2]~~by hand in a sink in the kitchen~~, and care for children. Today, most people have a choice about their choice of career. I feel fortunate to live in a time when I can follow my passion for computers, mathematics, and [3]~~learn about~~ the universe.

C Avoiding Plagiarism page 230

 4.4 page 231

1 Book: ⊙Ritsert Jansen.⊙ Funding Your Career in Science. ⊙2013⊙ New York: Cambridge University Press, Print.

Jansen, Ritsert. Funding Your Career in Science. New York: Cambridge University Press, **2013**. Print.

2 Magazine: Warner, Judith. New York Times Magazine. ⊙Print. "The Opt-Out Generation Wants Back In." 7 Aug. 2013: 34–38.⊙

Magazine: Warner, Judith. **"The Opt-Out Generation Wants Back In."** New York Times Magazine. 7 Aug. 2013: 34–38. **Print**.

3 Web article: "Coping with a Career Crisis." ⊙Sternberg, Robert. 27 Jan. 2014.⊙ Chronicle of Higher Education. Web. 15 Sept. 2014.

Web article: **Sternberg, Robert**. "Coping with a Career Crisis." Chronicle of Higher Education. **27 Jan. 2014**. Web. 15 Sept. 2014.

UNIT QUIZZES

NAME: ....

DATE: ....

Part A Academic Vocabulary

Circle the correct words to complete the sentences.

1 It is **optional / essential** for college students to complete all assignments.

2 Luis **informed / exchanged** Professor D'Amato that he would set up the class webpage.

3 There are several **trends / options** for the final class project. For example, students can create a marketing plan or design a webpage.

4 The college telephone directory allows students to **use / contact** each other easily.

5 A recent **trend / technology** among students is to use video calls to study with each other.

6 Amanda was happy to **inform / exchange** email addresses with her new classmate. Now they can help each other study.

7 James and Leo **used / informed** Professor Martin's study guide to prepare for the final exam.

8 Some professors do not like using **technology / options** and still grade papers by hand.

Part B Academic Collocations

Complete the paragraph with the correct academic collocations in the box.

essential tool	exchange messages	general trend	the best option	uses technology

Professor Scott gave her students helpful information on the first day of class. She said

.... for communicating with her was through email, not by telephone. She also
(1)

suggested that students .... with each other if they have questions about homework
(2)

assignments. Professor Scott said she .... every day in class. For example, she uses slide
(3)

presentations, videos, and the Internet for her lectures. She said that this is the ....
(4)

at the college, as almost all professors do the same thing. Professor Scott told her students that a notebook or

tablet computer was an .... for taking notes on her lectures, and recommended that
(5)

students bring them to the next class. At the end of the class, she wished her students luck for the semester.

NAME: ....

DATE: ....

Part A

Complete the sentences with the correct form of the verbs in parentheses.

1 People often .... their photos on social-media websites nowadays.
(share)

2 Smartphones .... great for communicating, surfing the Internet, and taking photos.
(be)

3 Professor Thompson .... her students to use their cell phones during class.
(not / allow)

4 Many teens .... movies on the computer rather than on TV.
(watch)

5 Leah .... a smartphone so she can video chat with her family.
(want)

6 I .... to talk with my friends instead of texting them.
(prefer)

7 We .... our work email on weekends.
(not / check)

8 Mauricio .... his old cell phone.
(not / like)

Part B

Correct the present-tense mistakes in the passage. There is one mistake in each sentence.

(1) Teens and young adults doesn't use Facebook as much as other social-media websites these days.
(2) People over age 50 uses Facebook more often than younger people. (3) They often adds photos of
their children, pets, or food. (4) Teens do not sometimes want to be friends with their parents on Facebook
because they want privacy. (5) Senior citizens are liking to use Facebook to reconnect with old friends.
(6) For them, it be a good way to stay in touch and share stories with friends from their past.

NAME: ....

DATE: ....

Part A

Complete the chart with the words and phrases from the box.

| book or magazine | information | Internet | words and ideas |

Ways to Avoid Plagiarism

Don't

1 Do not copy and paste sentences or paragraphs from the ....

2 Do not copy exact words from a ....

Do

1 Say where you found the ....

2 Use your own ....

Part B

Read each passage from an original text and the student texts below. Circle the type of plagiarism in each student text.

Original Passage:

In a recent study, Sylvia Moon, PhD, a professor of sociology at Tanner University, observed that people over the age of 60 are less likely to use text messaging to communicate. The older people she interviewed dislike this "abbreviated" way of communicating and prefer email or telephone calls. In fact, many are choosing to phone people rather than text them.

1 Student Text A:

   According to recent research, people over age 60 do not like to text message. They dislike that way of communicating and like to email or telephone instead. Usually, they call their friends instead of texting them.

   a This student did not say where the information came from.

   b This student cut and pasted sentences from the original passage.

2 Student Text B:

   According to Professor Sylvia Moon, people over the age of 60 are less likely to use text messaging to communicate. The older people she interviewed dislike this "abbreviated" way of communicating and prefer email or telephone calls. They are more likely to telephone rather than respond by text message.

   a This student did not say where the information came from.

   b This student cut and pasted sentences from the original passage.

Instructors: This is a list of possible prompts to assign as a unit writing quiz.

1 Is texting or using social-media sites such as Twitter and Facebook hurting people's ability to write well? Explain.

2 How can people use technology to raise money for a cause? Give examples.

3 Explain how small businesses can use technology to get more customers.

4 Do you think teachers should have to use technology in class? Why or why not?

5 Some people think online newspapers may completely replace traditional print newspapers. Do you think this would be a positive or negative change? Explain.

NAME: ....

DATE: ....

Part A Academic Vocabulary

Circle the correct words and phrases to complete the sentences.

1 Marita became a **successful / background** musician because she practiced every day.

2 The first **effort / priority** of many managers is to make sure that their employees are happy at work.

3 A lot of successful people make an **achievement / effort** to follow a plan every day.

4 Lawrence **analyzed / achieved** the data from his research. Then he shared it with his boss.

5 One **characteristic / background** of a good boss is to be a good listener.

6 Restaurant owners who have **an effort / a background** in business often do well.

7 The primary **achievement / goal** of Joe's Organic Food Company is to provide the best food and service to its customers.

8 Tim's greatest **achievement / effort** in school was graduating with high honors.

Part B Academic Phrases

Complete the paragraph with the correct academic phrases in the box.

it is important   one of the most important   part of the problem

.... factors for success is to find happiness in both one's work and home life.
         (1)
The happiest people are successful at work, and also enjoy hobbies such as going to the gym, spending

time with friends, or cooking after work. However, for many people .... is finding
                                                                                (2)
time to enjoy themselves after work because they are too tired. Even though it may be difficult,

.... to find time for enjoyable activities after work.
         (3)

NAME: ....

DATE: ....

Part A

Complete the sentences with the correct verb + preposition.

1 New employees can **learn from / take care of** their colleagues and managers.

2 Human-resource managers **get ahead / commit to** their employees' well-being at work.

3 Marcos wants to **look for / get ahead** in his company, so he is working on extra projects.

4 A successful company **focuses on / works for** employees, customers, and the products or services they sell.

5 TRH Corporation's day-care center **takes care of / learns from** the employees' young children.

6 Dale wants to **look for / commit to** a different job.

7 Janice would like to **work for / care about** herself instead of a big company.

8 Successful teachers **care about / look for** their students.

Part B

Correct the mistake in each sentence.

1 Successful business owners learn for their competition.

2 Marta's manager allows her to stay home to take care about her sick baby.

3 The ABC Toy Company wants to go ahead of the competition by making less expensive toys.

4 Heidi told her employees to look ways to improve customer service.

5 Leo likes to focus about answering emails first thing each morning.

6 The new manager is popular because he cares of his employees.

7 Anna committed with another year of teaching after she won the teacher of the year award.

8 Simone works on an animal-rescue organization while she studies to become a veterinarian.

NAME: ....

DATE: ....

Part A

Circle the best strategy for avoiding plagiarism for each student.

1 Ian doesn't have a lot of time to write. He thinks if he copies other writers' ideas it will save him time.

   a He should make a schedule to write every day.

   b He should read about the topic and talk about it with a friend in English.

   c He should get extra help at the writing center and ask a classmate to read his writing.

2 Jared doesn't have confidence in his writing skills. He thinks that using others' words will help his writing improve.

   a He should make a schedule to write every day.

   b He should read about the topic and talk about it with a friend in English.

   c He should get extra help at the writing center and ask a classmate to read his writing.

3 Tina thinks she doesn't know enough about the topic to write anything interesting in English. She thinks copying others' work will help her writing.

   a She should make a schedule to write every day.

   b She should read about the topic and talk about it with a friend in English.

   c She should get extra help at the writing center and ask a classmate to read her writing.

Part B

Match each strategy for avoiding plagiarism with the result.

Strategy

☐ 1 Read about your topic and discuss the ideas with someone in English.

☐ 2 Go to your school's writing center, or ask someone to read a draft of your ideas.

☐ 3 Make a writing schedule. Write a little bit every day.

Result

a This can help you improve your grade because you will improve your writing.

b You will have time to complete the assignment and decrease the pressure to meet deadlines.

c You will develop confidence in expressing your ideas.

Instructors: This is a list of possible prompts to assign as a unit writing quiz.

1 What is one goal you want to achieve? How will you achieve it?

2 Winston Churchill said, "Success consists of going from failure to failure without loss of enthusiasm." Do you agree with this statement? Why or why not? Explain.

3 Think of a successful person you know or admire. How did he or she become successful? What characteristics led to his or her success?

4 Think of a time you were successful at something, such as getting a good grade, or a job. What factors helped you succeed?

5 Think of a time when you were not successful at something. Why do you think you did not succeed? What did you learn from the experience?

NAME: ....   DATE: ....

Part A Academic Vocabulary

Circle the correct words to complete the paragraph.

Last year, my roommate Eric learned how one small change could make a big **improvement / attitude**
(1)
in his life. When Eric was younger, he was not very **relaxed / healthy**. He was overweight, and he was often
(2)
tired and sick. Eric's doctor advised him to start exercising. He began walking every day. Soon, he began
to have more **quality / energy** to do more physical activities, such as going dancing and gardening.
(3)
This surprised him. His **attitude / improvement** toward exercise changed. Today, he enjoys his daily walks,
(4)
dancing with his girlfriend, and working in the garden. He is also able to **produce / relax** more, and he
(5)
sleeps better at night. Eric feels that exercise has also been good for his **quality / brain** because he is able to
(6)
focus better on schoolwork. In fact, he is **relaxing / producing** better work in his classes than ever before.
(7)
Several of his professors have told him that the overall **quality / energy** of his assignments has improved.
(8)
His doctor's advice made a big change in Eric's life. He is now much healthier and happier.

Part B Academic Collocations

Complete the sentences with the correct form of the academic collocations in the box.

changed her attitude	high energy	positive attitude
quality of life	significant improvement	

1 Ana has a .... about life even though she had a difficult childhood.

2 Some people with .... do not need coffee in the morning to wake them up.

3 Most people have a better .... if they find work they love and make time for family,
   friends, and leisure activities.

4 After exercising for a month, Erin noticed a .... in her energy level.

5 Sonja .... about exercising after she lost five pounds.

NAME: ....

DATE: ....

Part A

Complete the sentences with the correct pronoun or possessive determiner.

1 Susie's doctor told her to change .... diet.

2 Lily bought .... new clothes because she lost 10 pounds recently.

3 The health center offers a weekly course on cooking healthy meals. .... has classes every Monday night.

4 Margo and Henry help .... with their new diet. They say it is much easier to diet with a friend.

5 Judith's eating habits are healthier than .... She never eats desserts, but I always do.

6 The nutrition professor told .... to cook a healthy meal for our final exam.

7 Steve bought lunch in the cafeteria because he forgot .... at home.

8 Sam joined the Elite Athletic Gym, and my brother and I joined the World Fitness Gym. Sam's gym is more popular, but .... is cheaper.

Part B

Correct the pronoun and possessive-determiner mistakes in the paragraph. There is one mistake in each sentence.

(1) Joseph he was gaining weight. He decided to take care of him and join a gym to start an exercise program. (2) The gym offered it's customers many exercise classes. (3) Last year, Joseph hurt the knee, so he had to be careful. (4) He took beginner yoga classes because their were easier. (5) After a month, Joseph felt stronger so began a weight-training program. (6) Joseph also changed her diet. (7) After six months, Joseph was very happy because lost 15 pounds.

NAME: ....

DATE: ....

Part A

Circle the type of common knowledge in each sentence.

1 President Franklin D. Roosevelt had polio.

   a common scientific fact

   b well-known person

2 Ebola is a very contagious disease.

   a common scientific fact

   b well-known historical event

3 Eating fewer calories will help you lose weight.

   a common scientific fact

   b well-known historical event

4 The Black Death, a highly contagious disease, killed millions of people in early 14th-century Europe.

   a common scientific fact

   b well-known historical event

5 Marie Curie was an important scientist in the early 20th century.

   a well-known historical event

   b well-known person

Part B

Check (✓) the sentences that are common knowledge.

☐ 1 A high fever and head or body aches are symptoms of the flu.

☐ 2 There were 3,697 flu-related deaths in 2013.

☐ 3 One way to avoid the flu is to wash your hands frequently.

☐ 4 Another way to prevent the flu is by getting a flu vaccine.

☐ 5 Jonas Salk and Thomas Francis developed the first flu vaccine in 1938.

☐ 6 Most people should get eight hours of sleep each night.

☐ 7 Coffee and other caffeinated foods can keep you awake at night.

☐ 8 About 30% of the population has trouble with sleeping.

☐ 9 If you don't get enough sleep, you may not be able to focus the next day.

☐ 10 The longest recorded time a person went without sleep is 18 days, 21 hours, and 40 minutes.

Instructors: This is a list of possible prompts to assign as a unit writing quiz.

1 Sometimes a small change can make a big difference in a person's health. Think of a small change that made a difference in your health or the health of someone you know. How did it make a big difference?

2 Early experiences, such as family meals or school gym classes, can influence people's health. Think of an early experience. What is an experience that has influenced your health habits? Describe how that experience influenced your health habits.

3 There are many popular diet trends these days. Have you or anyone you know followed one of these trends? Was it successful? Tell the story of your (or your friend's) experience with this diet trend.

4 Do you believe it is important to follow directions, such as from a doctor or bottle of medicine? Give an example of a time when you did (or did not) follow directions. What happened?

5 People use different things to help improve health, for example, websites, books, or social groups. Describe an experience you (or someone you know) had with one of these.

NAME: ....

DATE: ....

Part A Academic Vocabulary

Circle the correct words to complete the sentences.

1 Each employee is **key / responsible** for keeping his or her work area clean.

2 If things are difficult at work, try to stay **positive / obvious**. The next day is usually better.

3 Cynthia's **meeting / role** at the company is to train new employees.

4 It is **obvious / social** that Marion enjoys her work. She's always smiling.

5 Dean isn't a very **social / responsible** person at work. He prefers to work by himself.

6 The **key / role** to a successful business is to provide excellent products or services.

7 Everybody will be able to ask questions at the weekly **opportunities / meetings**.

8 Two years ago, Jon had the **opportunity / role** to buy his boss's shoe business. Now he is the happy owner of Hanson Shoes.

Part B Academic Phrases

Complete the paragraph with the correct form of the academic phrases in the box.

in order to	the first step	the process of

Carter and Elms, a company in Atlanta, Georgia, wanted to provide unemployed people in the community with good business clothes to wear on interviews. .... was to make a plan for the

(1)
project. The company employees then held an event .... collect good used business

(2)
clothing from employees and the community. After that, the employees invited unemployed people to try on the clothes. Everyone at Carter and Elms enjoyed .... planning the event, collecting

(3)
the clothes, and giving them to the unemployed.

NAME: ....

DATE: ....

Part A

Complete the paragraph with the imperative form of the correct verbs in the box.
Use the negative form when necessary.

apply	include	search	stay	worry
follow	proofread	send	update	write

If you are looking for a job, ... these steps. First, ...
                                                   (1)   **(2)**

your résumé with current work experience and educational achievements. ....
                                                                         (3)

your phone number and email address. Next, ... the Internet for available
                                                     (4)

jobs in your field. There are many job-search websites to help you. When you find a job you are

interested in, ... a cover letter explaining how you would be good at that job.
                                            (5)

.... your résumé and cover letter before you send them. ....
                  (6)   **(7)**

your documents to employers if they contain mistakes! Finally, remember that employers don't always call

or write back immediately. .... about it! .... for more jobs and
                                    (8)   **(9)**

.... positive. Good luck!
             (10)

Part B

Correct the four mistakes with imperatives in "Tips for New Employees." Use contractions
where possible.

Tips for New Employees

You follow these three tips when you start your job:

- Donot let a mistake at work discourage you.
- No be afraid to ask your boss for help if you need it.
- Finally, learn from the mistake and you do better next time.

NAME: .... **DATE:** ....

Part A

Write the two words or phrases from the box to use in a key-word search for each prompt.

business clothes	interview skills	styles for work
customer loyalty	résumés	successful department stores

1 Prompt: How can department stores keep their customers?

   Key words: ....

2 Prompt: What are employees wearing in today's workplace?

   Key words: ....

3 Prompt: Describe how to get a job.

   Key words: ....

Part B

Read each writing prompt. Cross out the least helpful key word or phrase for finding Internet sources.

1 Prompt: How can businesses help the hungry?

   a helping the hungry

   b food banks

   c growing food

2 Prompt: How can students find part-time summer jobs?

   a job-search tips

   b jobs after graduate school

   c part-time jobs for students

3 Prompt: What steps should someone take to learn a new computer skill?

   a learn an instrument

   b computer courses

   c learn software

Instructors: This is a list of possible prompts to assign as a unit writing quiz.

1 Think about something you know how to do, such as change a tire, write a computer program, or cook a meal. Describe how to complete the task. Use specific steps and clear examples.

2 What steps do you take when purchasing something online? Describe the process.

3 What steps should a student take to study for a test? Describe the process.

4 Describe the steps needed to get a good grade in this class. What is involved? Be specific and use clear examples.

5 Describe the steps in how to make friends in a new place. Be specific and give examples.

NAME: ....

DATE: ....

Part A Academic Vocabulary

Circle the correct words to complete the sentences.

1 Some teachers think it's useful to give students who get high grades a **connection / reward**.

2 It is **beneficial / educational** to meet as many classmates as you can when you start college.

3 With two years of job experience, Hugh has an **advantage / education** over the other job applicants.

4 Cultural-anthropology students learn about the **experience / connection** between language and culture.

5 Professor McKey **expected / explained** the answers to the difficult homework problems.

6 Maria studies hard because she thinks **education / reward** is very important.

7 Joshua has a lot of **advantage / experience** with computers. He wants to major in computer science.

8 College professors **expect / explain** their students to complete their homework assignments on time.

Part B Academic Collocations

Complete the paragraph with the academic collocations in the box.

close connection	gain experience	take advantage of
extremely beneficial	higher education	

    Extracurricular activities are school activities that students do outside of class. They are usually free

or inexpensive. Students do not get grades for them; they usually do them for fun. These activities are

common in middle schools, high schools, and places of .... such as colleges.
                            (1)

Some students .... these activities and participate in several of them at one time.
                (2)

For example, a student might join the Blogging Club, act in a school play, and compete on the swim team.

Working together creates a .... between the students. Participating in extra-curricular
                          (3)

activities is .... Students can ...., make new friends, and learn
        (4)   **(5)**

something new.

NAME: ....   **DATE:** ....

Part A

Circle the correct relative pronoun in each sentence.

1 Teaching Methods 101 is a course **that / who** all education majors have to take.

2 The GMAT is a exam **which / who** tests students applying to business school.

3 Dr. Granada is the professor **which / who** writes the education blog.

4 A serious college student is someone **who / which** asks good questions, listens carefully, and studies regularly.

5 A university is a school **that / who** offers bachelor's, master's, and doctoral degrees.

Part B

Correct the mistakes in the sentences. More than one answer may be possible.

1 Evan prefers a professor that explains the rules of grammar.

2 A bilingual dictionary is a dictionary who has words and definitions in two languages.

3 Students who needs to give a presentation in class must practice a lot.

4 A portfolio is a collection of student work that it assesses the student's general performance in a class.

5 Dr. Emil Chantal is the researcher wrote the textbook on modern education.

NAME: ....   DATE: ....

Part A

Complete the chart with words and phrases from the box.

| author's name | carefully | historically significant | paraphrase |
| background | exact words | main idea | unique wording |

What to Quote	How to Quote

• Choose quotes ....
  (1)
  There should not be too many quotes in your
  paragraph or essay.
 	
• Use quotes that support your
 	
  ....
        (2)
• Quote words, phrases, or sentences that:
 	
  • use .... or
           (3)
    unforgettable language, say something
    strong, dramatic, or moving
 	
  • include something that is memorable or
 	
    ....
            (4)
  • give an idea that is written very clearly or
 	
    hard to ....
              (5)
	• Write the ...., if known,
	                    (6)
	  in the same sentence as the quote.
	
	• Include information about the author's
	
	  .... if it is known.
	                (7)
	• Put the .... in quotation
	                  (8)
	  marks (" ").

Part B

Read the original text. Then read the student text and underline words that need quotes.

1 Original Passage (by Anne Ellsworth, President of Summers Education, Inc.):

We all know that education is necessary and a right. In fact, without quality education, children will not only be at a disadvantage in this country, but also in the global marketplace. We must act now: get our children the education they need and we will all benefit.

(CONTINUED)

Student Text:

According to Anne Ellsworth, President of Summers Education, all children should receive a high quality of education if they want to compete in the world's global economy. She says that it is necessary and a right, and that we must act now: get our children the education they need and we will all benefit.

2 Original Passage (by Christopher McArdle, Professor of English, Parker College):

My study showed that students who attend online-only classes feel less connected to their classmates than those students who take traditional face-to-face classes. However, those in hybrid classes – classes that are both online and face to face – feel even more connected than those in a traditional classroom course. In today's online world, we must adapt to this changing educational environment and take advantage of what technology has to offer. Hybrid classes are most definitely the way of the future.

Student Text:

English Professor Christopher McArdle of Parker College found in his study that students who are in traditional or online classes feel less connected to their classmates. On the other hand, those taking hybrid classes (mixed online and traditional classes) feel strongly connected to their classmates. In fact, McArdle says that in the modern world we must adapt to this changing educational environment and take advantage of what technology has to offer. He suggests that hybrid classes are most definitely the way of the future.

Instructors: This is a list of possible prompts to assign as a unit writing quiz.

1 Think about your educational experience. What does it mean to you to be a "good student"? Define it and give examples.

2 Many instructors teach using group work. Define group work and give examples.

3 Many students join study groups to help them study. What does a "study group" mean to you? Define it and give examples.

4 Define what a good education is to you. Give examples.

5 There are many kinds of assessment, such as tests, timed writings, and oral presentations. Choose one kind of assessment and define it. Give examples.

NAME: ....

DATE: ....

Part A Academic Vocabulary

Circle the correct words to complete the paragraph.

Central Park is a famous landmark in New York City. In the nineteenth **century / area**, the people of New
(1)

York State built the park at a **symbol / cost** of about ten million dollars. An American writer and an English
(2)

architect **represented / designed** the park. They wanted everyone to enjoy it. Today, the park has beautiful
(3)

lakes, gardens, playgrounds, and **areas / costs** for walking and running. There are many **cultural / religious**
(4)   (5)

events, such as rock concerts and art shows. The park has a castle, a skating rink, and several restaurants.

The park also has several statues, such as Balto and the Pilgrim. Balto the sled dog honors a dog in Alaska

that delivered medicine to sick children. The Pilgrim honors people who left a church in England and came

to the U.S. in the 1600s for **religious / cultural** freedom. There are many other things to do in Central Park.
(6)

It is easy find them if you have a good map. The **centuries / symbols** on the map show where things are.
(7)

For example, a knife and fork **designs / represents** a restaurant and the letter "i" means a place to
(8)

find information.

Part B Academic Phrases

Complete the paragraph with the correct academic phrases in the box.

a good example	another example	in addition to

Many famous structures that people made throughout the world are considered historical landmarks.

The Taj Mahal in India is .... of a famous great palace that is a landmark.
(1)

.... of a famous structure is the Great Wall of China. ....
(2)   (3)

these two ancient landmarks, Mount Rushmore in South Dakota, U.S., is another structure that shows

that humans can build huge, beautiful lasting structures.

NAME: ....   **DATE:** ....

Part A

Complete the paragraph with *there is* or *there are*.

From Northern Virginia to North Carolina, ... a national historic road called the

Blue Ridge Parkway. On the 469-mile road, ... many beautiful things to see, such as
(2)

Blue Ridge Mountain views and thick forests. .... also many picnic areas and campsites
(3)

near the Parkway. In Virginia, the Parkway travels through the countryside. ....
(4)

an old fence along the road. Signs let drivers know about historic sites on the Parkway. For example,

.... a sign for a historic cabin in Virginia. In North Carolina, ...
(5)   (6)

many forests and mountains. .... almost 300 places to stop and see beautiful views
(7)

on the beautiful Blue Ridge Parkway.

Part B

Correct the mistakes in the paragraph. There is one mistake in each sentence.

(1) They're many beautiful national parks to see in the United States. (2) For example, in Arizona, it is

a national park called the Grand Canyon. (3) There is many hiking trails in the Canyon. (4) In Everglades

National Park in Florida, there are a popular alligator farm. (5) They are over 2,000 alligators in the farm.

(6) In all, their are 59 U.S. National Parks for visitors to enjoy.

SCORE: .... / 9

NAME: ....

DATE: ....

Part A

Complete the chart with words and phrases from the box.

Internet	own ideas	own way
plagiarism	reuse	your friends

Sharing Ideas: Do's	Sharing Ideas: Don'ts
• Always use your .... (1) for writing assignments. Remember that your instructor wants to read your ideas, not the ideas of .... (2) • If you get a good idea from a friend during brainstorms, good! That's what brainstorms are for, BUT write the idea in your own words, and explain it in your .... (3)	• Don't .... your writing (4) assignments from other classes. Changing words or a few sentences is NOT acceptable. • Don't copy and paste ideas from papers by other students or from the .... This is (5) .... (6)

Part B

Read the student scenarios. Check the students who plagiarized.

☐ 1 Jill wrote a paragraph on the Grand Canyon. She asked her geology professor questions about the canyon. She used some of that information when she wrote her paragraph in her own words.

☐ 2 Chuck had to write a paragraph on the history of the Statue of Liberty. He wrote about it when he was in high school and got a good grade on that assignment. He thought he would reuse his old paragraph. He rewrote the topic and the concluding sentences.

☐ 3 Maddy met with her friends to brainstorm about her topic on Australia's Great Barrier Reef. Once she got some good information, she rewrote her paragraph using some of their ideas in her own words.

☐ 4 George wrote a paragraph about the history of the British flag. He didn't know anything about it, so he copied some information from the Internet for his paragraph. He wrote his own introduction.

☐ 5 Samantha wrote a paragraph about her city's new war memorial. She interviewed the mayor and recorded the interview. She used the mayor's words and ideas in her paragraph, but she did not write where she got the ideas.

☐ 6 Andrew wrote a paragraph about the best beaches in Florida to visit. He looked at his photos from his many visits to the state's beaches. Then he wrote descriptions based on his memories and old photos.

Instructors: This is a list of possible prompts to assign as a unit writing quiz.

1 Think of a landmark from your city or country. Describe it.

2 Think of a piece of art and describe it. Use details.

3 Describe the currency from your country.

4 Think of a popular place in your city. Describe it.

5 Think of a famous building in your city or country. Describe it.

NAME: ....

DATE: ....

Part A Academic Vocabulary

Circle the correct words to complete the sentences.

1 Good leaders consider others' **opinions / rights** when making decisions, even if they disagree.

2 Many people think that every citizen should have the **preference / right** to health care.

3 Many elderly people have **a preference / an individual** for reading print newspapers over online news.

4 Ms. Carter considers her students to be **individuals / adults**. She says they all have very different personalities and abilities.

5 Popular TV shows often **influence / appreciate** what teenagers say and do.

6 Teenagers do not always **appreciate / influence** what their parents teach them.

7 People who participate in **preferred / illegal** activities may go to jail.

8 Children often change their ideas when they become **adults / individuals**.

Part B Academic Collocations

Complete the sentences with the correct form of the academic collocations in the box.

directly influence	express an opinion	legal right
personal preference	strong preference	

1 The pop-music industry .... the fashion industry. Many people copy the clothes that their favorite pop musicians wear.

2 My .... is to listen to classical music. However, my co-workers like to listen to pop music all day.

3 Emma is very shy and does not like to .... in groups.

4 According to a recent survey, 67% of customers like to buy print books. Only 33% like to buy e-books. This shows that customers have a .... for buying print books.

5 All citizens should vote because it is their ....

NAME: .... DATE: ....

Part A

Complete the sentences with the superlative form of the adjective in parentheses.

1 .... way to learn good social behavior is through your parents.
  (good)

2 Living in another country is .... way to learn a second language.
  (fast)

3 Paella (a chicken and rice dish) was .... food Irene had in Spain.
  (delicious)

4 Joining an international chat group is .... way to make friends from other countries.
  (easy)

5 Meeting someone from another culture is .... way to learn about that culture.
  (interesting)

6 In his U.S. geography class, Hans learned that Hawaii is .... state.
  (wet)

7 Hans also discovered that Nevada is .... state.
  (dry)

8 In some cultures, family time – not work – is .... value.
  (important)

Part B

Correct the mistake in each sentence.

1 Some people think vegetarian diets are the most healthiest.

2 Safety is the bigest problem for children who share too much information online.

3 According to some experts, people in the happyest cultures find time for both work and leisure.

4 The most famousest movie stars like to have privacy.

5 The baddest way to handle a lot of email is to respond to it every hour.

SCORE: .... / 13

NAME: ....

DATE: ....

Part A

Complete the chart with words and phrases from the box.

capital letter	inside	lower-case	quotation marks
comma	introductory phrase	outside	

How to Quote
To introduce the person or source you are quoting: • Use an .... such as according to [name], or reporting words   (1)   such as argue, say, explain, ask.   • Put a .... after the phrase or reporting word.   (2)   • Use quotation marks around the quote.
To quote a whole sentence: • Include the .... and punctuation of the original quote inside   (3)   quotation marks.
To quote a phrase: • Use .... around the phrase.   (4)   • Start the quote with a .... letter, not a capital letter.   (5)   • The period of the whole sentence goes .... the closing   (6)   quotation mark.   • Question marks and exclamation points ending the whole sentence go   .... the closing quotation mark.   (7)

(CONTINUED)

Part B

Choose the quotation in each pair with correct punctuation and capitalization.

1 a Sims says Generally, young people want to follow what their friends do."

   b Sims says, "Generally, young people want to follow what their friends do."

2 a According to the government report on social programs, "Local organizations are beginning to help homeless people."

   b According to the government report on social programs "local organizations are beginning to help homeless people."

3 a In her speech, Ms. Paige said teachers are not always, "aware of how they affect students".

   b In her speech, Ms. Paige said teachers are not always "aware of how they affect students."

4 a The mayor exclaimed "Thank you, volunteers, for coming out to help today!"

   b The mayor exclaimed, "Thank you, volunteers, for coming out to help today"!

5 a As researcher Jonathan Speck asks, "Should company presidents receive such high pay"?

   b As researcher Jonathan Speck asks, "should company presidents receive such high pay?

6 a Professor Saunders argues that "more funding is needed."

   b Professor Saunders argues that "More funding is needed"

Instructors: This is a list of possible prompts to assign as a unit writing quiz.

1 Do you think celebrities make too much money? Explain.

2 Should governments have more control over what appears on the Internet? Explain.

3 Should teachers' salaries be based on how much their students learn? Provide reasons.

4 Do you think parents who stay at home to care for young children should receive money from the government? Why or why not?

5 Should people limit the amount of time they use social-media sites such as Facebook or Twitter? Why or why not?

NAME: ....

DATE: ....

Part A Academic Vocabulary

Circle the correct words to complete the sentences.

1 Mina's boss trusts her because she is **powerful / honest**.

2 Max's award was the **result / security** of years of hard work.

3 Thirty years ago, people often had the same job for most of their lives. Today, there is not the same level of job **objectives / security**.

4 An education gives people the **result / power** to get good jobs.

5 Carlos **decided / performed** to become a zookeeper when he visited the zoo at age 10.

6 Sara loves to **discover / decide** new foods and cultures in her job as a tour guide.

7 A hotel concierge **decides / performs** such tasks as answering questions, making dinner reservations, and recommending places to visit.

8 Olivia's career **objective / result** is to become a lawyer.

Part B Academic Phrases

Complete the paragraph with the correct form of the academic phrases in the box.

a type of	in general	in particular

Jessica wanted to find the perfect career. She asked her college advisor for help. They had a

long discussion. Jessica said she wants .... job where she can help people.
                                                                                          (1)

...., she wants to help poor people succeed. ...., she wants to
              (2)   (3)

help homeless people find housing and jobs. The advisor suggested that Jessica apply for a job at the local

homeless shelter. Now she is the housing coordinator, and she is very happy.

NAME: ....   DATE: ....

Part A

Circle the correct words and phrases to make sentences with parallel structure.

1 Steven likes collecting stamps, reading books, and ....
   a ride his bike
   b riding his bike
   c to ride his bike

2 Tamara's clothing is beautiful, unique, and ....
   a inexpensive
   b costs less
   c inexpensive to buy

3 To improve his grades, Rico decided to study with classmates, talk to professors, and
   ....
   a doing better on tests
   b does better on tests
   c do better on tests

4 Gina's responsibilities as a nurse include taking care of patients and ....
   a comfort families
   b comforting families
   c make families comfortable

Part B

Correct the error with parallel structure in each sentence.

1 College graduates can go to graduate school, find jobs, or some might want to travel.

2 A good kindergarten teacher is friendly, patient, and has a lot of creativity.

3 Successful businesses have excellent management, strong customer service, and offer good employee benefits.

4 A good boss is respectful, treats employees fairly, and kind.

5 Jones-Wyatt University offers courses in economics, history, and how to speak Spanish.

6 Jeremiah wants to spend the summer reading books, exercising three mornings each week, and going to the beach.

NAME: ....

DATE: ....

Part A

Label the underlined part of the sources in each citation with words and phrases from the box.

article title	date of publication	medium	publication title
city of publication	date you read article	page number	publisher

1 **Book**

Covey, Stephen R. *The 7 Habits of Highly Effective People: Powerful Lessons in Personal Change.*

<u>New York</u>: <u>Simon & Schuster</u>. Anniversary Ed. 2013. Print

2 **Newspaper**

White, Ronald. "<u>Raising the Bar on Management.</u>" *Los Angeles Times* 21 June 2015: <u>C3</u>. Print.

3 **Magazine**

Harkinson, Josh. "The Tech Industry Has a Giant Diversity Problem."<u>*Mother Jones*</u>

<u>July–August 2015</u>: 25–28. Print.

4 **Web Article**

McCord, Sara. "How to Ask for Help at a New Job." *Newsweek* 14 Sept. 2014. <u>Web</u>. <u>21 June 2015</u>.

Part B Strategies Examples

Choose the Works Cited entry in each pair with the correctly ordered information.

1 **Book**

a Leibman, Peter P. *Launch a Teaching Career: Secrets for Aspiring Teachers.* Rowman & Littlefield. Lanham, MD, 2015. Print.

b Leibman, Peter P. *Launch a Teaching Career: Secrets for Aspiring Teachers.* Lanham, MD: Rowman & Littlefield, 2015. Print.

2 **Newspaper**

a Fox, Tom. "Anxiety Is a Good Attribute for Leaders." *Los Angeles Times* 14 June 2015: C7. Print.

b "Anxiety Is a Good Attribute for Leaders." Fox, Tom. *Los Angeles Times* 14 June 2015: C7. Print.

3 **Magazine**

a Kaufman, Dan. "Fate of the Union." *New York Times Magazine* 14 June 2015: 41–45. Print.

b Kaufman, Dan. "Fate of the Union." *New York Times Magazine*: 41–45. 14 June 2015. Print.

4 **Web Article**

a Ibarra, Herminia. "Assessment: Is It Time to Rethink Your Career?" *Harvard Business Review*. 17 June 2015. 20 June 2015. Web.

b Ibarra, Herminia. "Assessment: Is It Time to Rethink Your Career?" *Harvard Business Review*. 17 June 2015. Web. 20 June 2015.

Instructors: This is a list of possible prompts to assign as a unit writing quiz.

1 What influenced your choice of area of study or major? Give reasons and details.

2 Think of a person you admire. Write about three values you think this person has. Give examples and explain.

3 Think about someone who has chosen a career they love. Explain the person's career, his or her reasons for choosing it, and his or her experience with it.

4 Think of three jobs you would like to have. Explain what they are and why you would like to have them.

5 Think of three jobs you would *not* like to have. Explain what they are and why you wouldn't like to have them.

UNIT QUIZZES ANSWER KEY

UNIT 1

Unit 1 Vocabulary

Part A
1 essential
2 informed
3 options
4 contact
5 trend
6 exchange
7 used
8 technology

Part B
1 the best option
2 exchange messages
3 uses technology
4 general trend
5 essential tool

Unit 1 Grammar

Part A
1 share
2 are
3 doesn't allow (does not allow)
4 watch
5 wants
6 prefer
7 don't check (do not check)
8 doesn't like (does not like)

Part B

(1) Teens and young adults ~~doesn't~~ *don't* use Facebook as much as other social-media websites these days. (2) People over age 50 ~~uses~~ *use* Facebook more often than younger people. (3) They often ~~adds~~ *add* photos of their children, pets, or food. (4) Teens do not ~~sometimes~~ want to be friends with their parents *sometimes*^ on Facebook because they want privacy. (5) Senior citizens ~~are liking~~ *like* to use Facebook to reconnect with old friends. (6) For them, it ~~be~~ *is* a good way to stay in touch and share stories with friends from their past.

Unit 1 Avoiding Plagiarism

Part A
Don'ts
1 Internet
2 book or magazine
Do's
1 information
2 words and ideas

Part B
1 a
2 b

UNIT 2

Unit 2 Vocabulary

Part A
1 successful
2 priority
3 effort
4 analyzed
5 characteristic
6 a background
7 goal
8 achievement

Part B
1 One of the most important
2 part of the problem
3 it is important

Unit 2 Grammar

Part A
1 learn from
2 commit to
3 get ahead
4 focuses on
5 takes care of
6 look for
7 work for
8 care about

Part B

1 Successful business owners learn ~~for~~ *from* their competition.

2 Marta's manager allows her to stay home to take care ~~about~~ *of* her sick baby.

3 The ABC Toy Company wants to ~~go~~ *get* ahead of the competition by making less expensive toys.

4 Heidi told her employees to look *for* ^ ways to improve their customer service.

5 Leo likes to focus ~~about~~ *on* answering emails first thing each morning.

6 The new manager is popular because he cares ~~of~~ *about* his employees.

7 Anna committed ~~with~~ *to* another year of teaching after she won the teacher of the year award.

8 Simone works ~~on~~ *for* an animal-rescue organization while she studies to become a veterinarian.

Unit 2 Avoiding Plagiarism

Part A

1 a
2 c
3 b

Part B

1 c
2 a
3 b

UNIT 3

Unit 3 Vocabulary

Part A

1 improvement
2 healthy
3 energy
4 attitude
5 relax
6 brain
7 producing
8 quality

Part B

1 positive attitude
2 high energy
3 quality of life
4 significant improvement
5 changed her attitude

Unit 3 Grammar

Part A

1 her
2 herself
3 It
4 each other
5 mine
6 us
7 his
8 ours

Part B

(1) Joseph ~~he~~ was gaining weight. He decided to take care of ~~him~~ *himself* and join a gym to start an exercise program. (2) The gym offered ~~it's~~ *its* customers many exercise classes. (3) Last year, Joseph hurt ~~the~~ *his* knee, so he had to be careful. (4) He took beginner yoga classes because ~~their~~ *they* were easier. (5) After a month, Joseph felt stronger so *he* ^ began a weight-training program. (6) Joseph also changed ~~her~~ *his* diet. (7) After six months, Joseph was very happy because *he* ^ lost 15 pounds.

Unit 3 Avoiding Plagiarism

Part A

1 b
2 a
3 a
4 b
5 b

Part B

Check: 1, 3, 4, 6, 7, 9

UNIT 4

Unit 4 Vocabulary

Part A
1 responsible
2 positive
3 role
4 obvious
5 social
6 key
7 meetings
8 opportunity

Part B
1 The first step
2 in order to
3 the process of

Unit 4 Grammar

Part A
1 follow
2 update
3 Include
4 search
5 write
6 Proofread
7 Don't send
8 Don't worry
9 Apply
10 stay

Part B
Follow
~~You follow~~ these suggestions when you start
your job:
Don't
• ~~Donot~~ let a mistake at work discourage you.
Don't
• ~~No~~ be afraid to ask your boss for help if you
  need it.

• Finally, learn from the mistake and ~~you~~ do
  better next time.

Unit 4 Avoiding Plagiarism

Part A
1 customer loyalty, successful department stores
2 business clothes, styles for work
3 résumés, interview skills

Part B
1 c
2 b
3 a

UNIT 5

Unit 5 Vocabulary

Part A
1 reward
2 beneficial
3 advantage
4 connection
5 explained
6 education
7 experience
8 expect

Part B
1 higher education
2 take advantage of
3 close connection
4 extremely beneficial
5 gain experience

Unit 5 Grammar

Part A
1 that
2 which
3 who
4 who
5 that

Part B
1 Evan prefers a professor ~~that~~ *who* explains the rules
  of grammar.
2 A bilingual dictionary is a dictionary ~~who~~ *that/which* has
  words and definitions in two languages.
3 Students who ~~needs~~ *need* to give a presentation in
  class must practice a lot.
4 A portfolio is a collection of student work that
  ~~it~~ assesses the student's general performance in
  a class.
5 Dr. Emil Chantal is the researcher *who* wrote the
  textbook on modern education.

Unit 5 Avoiding Plagiarism

Part A
1 carefully
2 main idea
3 unique wording
4 historically significant
5 paraphrase
6 author's name
7 background
8 exact words

Part B
1 According to Anne Ellsworth, President of Summers Education, all children should receive a high quality of education if they want to compete in the world's global economy. She says that it is necessary and a right, and that we must act now: get our children the education they need and we will all benefit.
2 English Professor Christopher McArdle of Parker College found in his study that students who are in traditional or online classes feel less connected to their classmates. On the other hand, those taking hybrid classes (mixed online and traditional classes) feel strongly connected to their classmates. In fact, McArdle says that in the modern world we must adapt to this changing educational environment and take advantage of what technology has to offer. He suggests that hybrid classes are most definitely the way of the future.

UNIT 6

Unit 6 Vocabulary

Part A
1 century
2 cost
3 designed
4 areas
5 cultural
6 religious
7 symbols
8 represents

Part B
1 a good example
2 Another example
3 In addition to

Unit 6 Grammar

Part A
1 there is
2 there are
3 There are
4 There is
5 there is
6 there are
7 There are

Part B
(1) ~~They're~~ *There are* many beautiful national parks to see in the United States. (2) For example, in Arizona, ~~it~~ *there* is a national park called the Grand Canyon. (3) There ~~is~~ *are* many hiking trails in the Canyon. (4) In Everglades National Park in Florida, there ~~is~~ are a popular alligator farm. (5) ~~They~~ *There* are over 2,000 alligators in the farm. (6) In all, ~~their~~ *there* are 59 National Parks for visitors to enjoy.

Unit 6 Avoiding Plagiarism

Part A
1 own ideas
2 your friends
3 own way
4 reuse
5 Internet
6 plagiarism

Part B
Check: 2, 4, 5

UNIT 7

Unit 7 Vocabulary

Part A
1 opinions
2 right
3 a preference
4 individuals
5 influence
6 appreciate
7 illegal
8 adults

Part B

1 directly influences
2 personal preference
3 express her opinion
4 strong preference
5 legal right

Unit 7 Grammar

Part A

1 The best
2 the fastest
3 the most delicious
4 the easiest
5 the most interesting
6 the wettest
7 the driest
8 the most important

Part B

1 Some people think vegetarian diets are the
~~most~~ healthiest.

2 Safety is the *biggest* ~~bigest~~ problem for children who
share too much information online.

3 According to some experts, people in the
happiest ~~happyest~~ cultures find time for both work and
leisure.

4 The most *famous* ~~famousest~~ movie stars like to have
privacy.

5 The *worst* ~~baddest~~ way to handle a lot of email is to
respond to it every hour.

Unit 7 Avoiding Plagiarism

Part A

1 introductory phrase
2 comma
3 capital letter
4 quotation marks
5 lower-case
6 inside
7 outside

Part B

1 b
2 a
3 b
4 b
5 a
6 a

UNIT 8

Unit 8 Vocabulary

Part A

1 honest
2 result
3 security
4 power
5 decided
6 discover
7 performs
8 objective

Part B

1 a type of
2 In general
3 In particular

Unit 8 Grammar

Part A

1 b　　　　2 a　　　　3 c　　　　4 b

Part B

1 College graduates can go to graduate school,
find jobs, or ~~some might want to~~ *travel*.

2 A good kindergarten teacher is friendly, patient,
and *creative* ~~has a lot of creativity~~.

3 Successful businesses have excellent
management, strong customer service, and
~~offer~~ good employee benefits.

4 A good boss is respectful, ~~treats employees~~
~~fairly~~ *fair*, and kind.

5 Jones-Wyatt University offers courses in
economics, history, and ~~how to speak Spanish~~ *Spanish*.

6 Jeremiah wants to spend the summer reading
books, exercising ~~three mornings each week~~,
and going to the beach.

Unit 8 Avoiding Plagiarism

Part A

1 Book

Covey, Stephen R. *The 7 Habits of Highly*

Effective People: Powerful Lessons in Personal
      city of
      publication   *publisher*
Change. <u>New York</u>: <u>Simon & Schuster</u>.

Anniversary Ed. 2013. Print

2 Newspaper
                      article title
White, Ronald. <u>"Raising the Bar on Management."</u>
                    page number
Los Angeles Times 21 June 2015: <u>C3</u>. Print.

3 Magazine

Harkinson, Josh. "The Tech Industry Has a
                  publication title
Giant Diversity Problem." <u>*Mother Jones*</u>
date of publication
<u>July–August 2015</u>: 25–28. Print.

4 Web Article

McCord, Sara. "How to Ask for Help at a
                    medium
New Job." *Newsweek* 14 Sept. 2014. <u>Web</u>.
date you read article
  <u>21 June 2015</u>.

Part B

1 b   2 a   3 a   4 b

UNIT QUIZZES WRITING RUBRIC

Final Draft Writing Assignment Rubric

CATEGORY	CRITERIA	SCORE
Language Use	Grammar and vocabulary are accurate, appropriate, and varied. Sentence types are varied and used appropriately. Level of formality (register) shows a good understanding of audience and purpose. Mechanics (capitalization, punctuation, indentation, and spelling) are strong.	
Organization & Mode (structure)	Writing is well organized and follows the conventions of academic writing: • Paragraph – topic sentence, supporting details, concluding sentence • Essay – introduction with thesis, body paragraphs, conclusion Rhetorical mode is used correctly and appropriately. Research is clearly and correctly integrated into student writing (if applicable).	
Coherence, Clarity, & Unity	Sentences within a paragraph flow logically with appropriate transitions; paragraphs within an essay flow logically with appropriate transitions. Sentences and ideas are clear and make sense to the reader. All sentences in a paragraph relate to the topic sentence; all paragraphs in an essay relate to the thesis.	
Content & Development (meaning)	Writing completes the task and fully answers the prompt. Content is meaningful and interesting. Main points and ideas are fully developed with good support and logic.	

How well does the response meet the criteria?	Recommended Score
At least 90%	25
At least 80%	20
At least 70%	15
At least 60%	10
At least 50%	5
Less than 50%	0
Total Score Possible per Section	25
Total Score Possible	100

Feedback: